Sit, Stand, Walk, Run: A Vocabulary for the Christian's Journey

Gordon S. Jackson

M☩ Zion Ridge Press
Books Off the Beaten Path

www.MtZionRidgePress.com

Mt Zion Ridge Press LLC
295 Gum Springs Rd, NW
Georgetown, TN 37366

https://www.mtzionridgepress.com

ISBN 13: 978-1-962862-72-1

Published in the United States of America
Publication Date: June 15, 2025

Copyright: © 2024 Gordon S. Jackson

Editor-In-Chief: Michelle Levigne
Executive Editor: Tamera Lynn Kraft

Cover art design by Tamera Lynn Kraft
Cover Art Copyright by Mt Zion Ridge Press LLC © 2025

Table of Contents

Part 3: Wrapping Up

Introduction: Spiritual Mobility

Imagine you're on a 1,000-mile car trip. It's almost certainly going to be filled with more variety than you realize. Yes, much of the time you might be going sixty-five or seventy miles per hour (or maybe a bit faster); many of those thousand miles will consist of routine, predictable driving. But then you will on occasion hit heavy traffic or bad weather that will slow you down. Or road construction that will stop you completely.

You and your passengers will take numerous rest stops and perhaps you'll even break up the journey by spending a night with relatives or friends along the way. Much of the journey, you can anticipate. But then come the unexpected moments: a flat tire, a skid on an icy road, or your child warning he's about to throw up because of car sickness. There's a plus side too, with that amazing sunset you see or that brilliantly lit golden field of wheat.

Come to think of it, your road trip is not unlike your Christian walk. Your faith journey, while routine much of the time and seemingly the same day after day, is in fact broken up in various ways: times when your faith is sorely tested, perhaps, or a spiritual "high" like the one you experienced at that couples retreat last summer. Or some unexplained flatness in your faith journey when everything at church, your Bible reading and prayer life seem blah. It's as if you've hit road construction on your journey.

Philosopher and theologian Peter Kreeft says that "The image of life as a road is probably the single most popular image in the world's literature."[1] And, he might have added, the world's religions.

Referring to the Christian faith, Walter Brueggemann writes that "The metaphor of journey or sojourn is a radical one. It is a challenge to the dominant ideologies of our time which yearn for settlement, security and placement." He continues: "The metaphor of journey as a way of speaking about faith is utilized by the New Testament in various ways." These include Christian discipleship as following "the way."[2]

~~~~~

Roads are built for dissatisfied people: all those you'll see on the road tomorrow, whether they're in a car, on a bike or on foot, they're not content with where they are and want to be somewhere else. The

---

[1] Peter Kreeft: *The Journey: A Spiritual Roadmap for Modern Pilgrims*, 11.
[2] Walter Brueggemann: *Genesis*, 122.

exception might be someone who's only out for a drive or a run. For the most part, though, people are en route to somewhere else. They're on a journey. Perhaps it's short, like a quick trip to the store, or maybe a longer commute to the office. These days we have the advantage of amazingly fast travel that our forebears could not have imagined, with a flight from New York cross-country to Los Angeles taking about five hours. Compare that with the four to six months it would have taken nineteenth century pioneers to complete that trip.

The Bible is full of journeys, none of them courtesy of American Airlines, Delta or United. By contrast, biblical characters undertook their journeys by foot or perhaps by donkey. This "radical metaphor" of journeys appears repeatedly in Scripture. We can make at least six generalizations about the characters who undertook them and their travels.

First, is the diverse character of biblical journeys. We have journeys of obedience to God's explicit command (Abraham leaving for the Promised Land, Gideon going down to the Midianite camp), as well as ones of disobedience. Think of Jonah.

Some journeys culminate in enlightenment, as with Peter, James and John witnessing the transfiguration, or Paul's Damascus Road experience. Some are evangelistic, as with Paul's subsequent missionary journeys, while others (typically in the Old Testament) are prophetic, when Yahweh's servants speak His truth to power.

Yet others are steeped in risk, as when Queen Esther approaches the king without his permission, a move that could lead to severe punishment, even death, if he were having a bad hair day. Or in Acts we read of the disciple in Damascus, Ananias, whom God instructs to go and visit the now-blinded Paul, the one who has come to hunt down Christians.

Second, whatever their character, most of these journeys were voluntary. Even Jesus' journey to Jerusalem and what He knew would be certain death was taken voluntarily, in accordance with His Father's will. Others, though, were not. Think of the plight of Joseph, sold into slavery by his brothers and taken to Egypt. (Gen. 37) Similarly, there's the young Israelite girl captured by the Syrians on one of their raids, who ends up in the house of Naaman: a Syrian general who contracts leprosy. (2 Ki. 5) This young girl, who is never identified by name, tells her master of the prophet who she believes will heal Naaman, which he does — the outcome of a young girl's journey made under duress. By far the majority of journeys in the Bible, however, are by people acting of their own volition.

A **third** theme is that, as we see with Joseph's story and that of the Israelite maid, and so many others, their journeys in some significant ways advance God's Kingdom. That is especially the case with Jesus heading toward His crucifixion. The travelers whose journeys are described in

Scripture generally have little grasp of how much they are furthering God's Kingdom and purposes. Abraham, for instance, could not have understood how much his faithfulness in leaving Ur would shape world history. Similarly, Moses, in taking that short journey to investigate a bush that wouldn't stop burning, could not have begun to realize what God had in store for him. (Ex. 3) Or consider Ruth, unhesitatingly leaving her Moabite home and culture to go with her mother-in-law to Naomi's hometown and consequently becoming part of Jesus' lineage. (Ru. 1)

Fourth, biblical journeys were typically undertaken under grueling conditions. They were also lengthy, comparable to the pioneers whose wagons on the Oregon Trail would take them fifteen miles a day, twenty if conditions were good. Journeying in Bible times was never taken lightly. Dusty roads, or even non-existent ones, coupled with Middle Eastern heat and the threat of bandits, meant nobody was a tourist in the way we think of a certain category of travelers today. People didn't undertake journeys for the fun of it. We can be sure that Joseph and a heavily pregnant Mary didn't set out for Bethlehem excited at the prospect of seeing that town's sights and eating at some of its best restaurants. (Lk. 2:1-7) Nor would the couple, now with an infant, welcome the disruption when an angel told them to get out of town, fast, because the forces of evil threatened the life of baby Jesus. (Mt. 2:13-15) Their hurried trip to Egypt, we can be sure, was not undertaken in great comfort. Likewise, the experiences of Noah and his family were not even remotely comparable to a Royal Caribbean cruise. (Gen. 6:9-8:19) Besides being fed and entertained, modern day cruise passengers know their destination and have the option of getting off when they like.

We have numerous examples too of travel being actually hazardous. Paul was shipwrecked (Acts 27:27-44), Jonah was thrown overboard (Jon. 1), and in Jesus' parable the good Samaritan helped a man who had fallen victim to bandits. (Lk. 10:25-37)

These last three examples point to a **fifth** theme, that not all intended journeys are completed. Even when we set out to honor God's will, things don't always turn out as expected. Take Peter's aborted attempt to walk to Jesus on the water, for example. (Mt. 14:22-33) Then there's Paul's vision of a man from Macedonia, telling him to change course and come over and bring the gospel to the Macedonians. (Acts 16:9) So Paul abandons his original destination for a new one.

That leads us to our **sixth** theme: The best journeys are those clearly shaped by God's leading. Whether it is Peter obeying the Spirit's leading and journeying to share the gospel with Cornelius, (Acts 10) or Moses making repeated trips to Pharoah's court (Ex. 7-12), godly men and women throughout the ages have in effect prayed the prayer of Charles Spurgeon: "Lord, let me go where Thou leadest, on Thy errands, under

Thy command, and in the power of Thy Spirit."[3]

~~~~~

Notwithstanding the routine aspects of the Christian life, we all encounter lots more "road conditions" than we may realize. That's exactly what the Bible tells us to expect. This book explores those ups and downs, stops and starts, of the Christian walk. We'll do so by exploring a number of concepts that speak to our "posture" or "status" at any given moment.

Among these are times when we are to:

- **Sit**, perhaps when we are at rest, or waiting for God to show us the next steps in our walk with Him;
- **Stand**, when getting ready for action or needing to take a stand for or against something as a Christian;
- **Walk**, a seemingly routine activity but crucial in moving us forward in our faith, and
- **Run**, as in running the good race of which Paul speaks, when we are at peak performance in living out our faith.[4]

It's time to introduce the idea that undergirds all these concepts: mobility. Or, for our purposes, "spiritual mobility," which we will define as our ability to "move forward unhindered in our Christian journeys." Ordinary mobility, according to the Harvard University Medical School, is

> ... *defined as your ability to move purposefully as you go through your day. It is the foundation for living a healthy and independent life. Mobility comprises all the skills required for everyday living: physical stamina, strength, balance, coordination, and range of motion. The importance of mobility becomes clear when you rise out of bed, shower, manage a flight of stairs, walk a half-mile, get in and out of a car, or carry groceries... In short, mobility helps you stay "in the game."*[5]

Many passages in Scripture refer to our physical mobility. But a passage in Deuteronomy reminds us that all our movement ultimately rests upon our faith, as Moses tells the Israelites: "Fix these words of mine in your hearts and minds; tie them as symbols on your hands and bind them on your foreheads. Teach them to your children, talking about them when you sit at home and when you walk along the road, when you lie down and when you get up." (Dt. 11:18-19) Note *sit* at home, *walk* along the road, *lie down*, and *get up*. That's a pretty comprehensive range of our movements. In other words, *whatever* our posture, Moses says God's

---

[3] https://ccel.org/ccel/spurgeon/checkbook.xi.html. Accessed May 20, 2024.
[4] 2 Tim. 4:7.
[5] https://www.health.harvard.edu/topics/mobility. Accessed April 29, 2024.

instructions should be in our hearts and minds. That commitment to adhering constantly to God's word and direction is the thread that runs throughout this book, as we'll look at positions like **Sitting**, **Walking** and **Getting Up**, and a host of others. As we will see, the various aspects of our spiritual journey, its highs and lows, its blessings and challenges, require a spiritual flexibility and suppleness that neatly parallel the physical mobility of which the Harvard definition spoke.

~~~~~

Paul Tournier says, "The Holy Spirit is always calling us forward, not back."[6] With our Christian lives, then, God expects us to be moving forward (with an exception or two along the way). Not surprisingly, with a little effort we can tease out of Scripture what we can call a "vocabulary for the journey." To whet your appetite, think of the times in Scripture you encounter Jesus telling His followers about **Following**, or **Departing** or **Being Still**. Each of these concepts speaks to some aspect of our Christian life and our relationship to God at any given moment.

There is much general guidance or advice in Scripture on how we should live our lives. Jesus' parables alone offer great wisdom and direction for His followers. To make these lessons more immediately applicable to our lives, however, our emphasis will instead be on those instances in Scripture when God deals with individuals. For example, there's the well-known call of Moses and the burning bush, when God speaks to him: "So now, go, I am sending you to Pharaoh...." (Ex. 3:16) God expects Moses to obey by going. In the New Testament, Jesus calls Lazarus from the tomb: "Lazarus, come out." (Jn. 11:43) Again, we have a personalized command, this time an extraordinary direction to a dead man to return to life and rejoin the living world. Some of the concepts we will examine occur frequently, such as **Walking** and **Standing**. Others occur less often, such as **Fleeing** or **Soaring**. Yet even these less frequently mentioned ideas offer us rich insights for our journey.

An important caveat is in order. Please do not regard these reflections as formal theological or exhaustive analyses. The Scriptures that illustrate each reflection are only a small sampling of those I could have chosen. Indeed, it might have been possible to rely on an entirely different set of Bible passages to make the points I have. A skeptic may view this particular selection of Bible passages as cherry picking to illustrate each selection. However, I regard these verses instead as a springboard from which each selection arises, with the goal of identifying themes pertinent to the Christian journey. You will no doubt think of other Scriptures that could be added. That's good. By referring to them to supplement each reflection, you will make your encounter with this material more

---

[6] Paul Tournier: *The Adventure of Living*, 40.

illuminating. Also, the insights that follow may occasionally interpret Scripture differently from your own understanding. If that occurs, feel free to rely on your understanding of these Bible passages. But please don't let any such differences distract you from a reflection's main points.

~~~~~

Some words on wording are in order. All scripture references are from the *New International Version* of the Bible, except where noted otherwise. Then there is the issue of inclusive language. Some quotes use "man," "mankind" and so on when referring to people in general. These quotes reflect earlier usage which characterizes contemporary English less and less. To present all sources as accurately as possible, I have included these entries with their original wording.[7] One other thing regarding wording: I use "chapter" to refer to the Scripture readings. To avoid confusion, I will refer to the chapters in this book as "reflections."

This series of reflections can enrich your Christian journey in at least three ways. They are *understanding*, *acting*, and *relating*. First, there's the inherent value of an expanded vocabulary. Imagine that I have a severe rash on my arms; to me, it's a troubling, itchy irritation. To my doctor, it could be any of a dozen conditions, each of which has a name and needs a particular treatment. His vocabulary enables an accurate diagnosis and treatment plan. His training should provide the understanding needed to treat my condition. I'd be worried if all he could say is, "Looks like a rash to me."

Like doctors, architects, police officers and others engaged in specialized activities, theologians too have their own specialized vocabulary. But ordinary lay people like you and me don't have to have formal training in theology to benefit from knowing and using the "journey-related" terms in this book.

Having a richer vocabulary that describes our Christian journey enables us better to understand our ever-deepening relationship with God our Father. Knowing the nuanced difference between **Detours** and **Stumbling and Falling**, for example, can be significant. And how is **Go!** different from **Getting Up**? And why does it matter?

Second, there's the diagnostic role mentioned above, which when necessary should lead to *acting*. For instance, an expanded terminology

---

[7] The use of masculine pronouns to refer to God is done with due deference to concerns about inclusive language. Their use is not to assert that God is masculine. Where possible, attempts have been made to avoid masculine pronouns. But they have been included rather than resort to the heavy-handed artificiality of writing things like "We seek to know who God is, how God deals with us, and what God wants to characterize our life together as God's people." Elsewhere, quoted material using these pronouns is left unchanged, respecting the need to accurately present these sources.

can help you to understand that being in a spiritual slump, for example, is a frequent (although unwelcome) aspect of Christian living, something you may need to address by talking your condition through with someone. Or at times **Fleeing** from a situation may be the wisest course for you. A diagnostic application of these reflections can help you know how to respond to your current situation. It's been said that wisdom is simply knowing what to do next. But to act wisely first requires an accurate assessment of your current situation. Knowing that you're in **Waiting** mode, for instance, reminds you to be patient until God's will for your next step becomes clear. Or perhaps you should be **Checking the Map**. Simply having a concrete term to identify your situation is helpful in taking a well-informed next step.

The third benefit is the usefulness of this vocabulary in *relating* to others. While the concepts on the following pages apply to *your* walk, so too are they helpful for you to empathize with other Christians, where *they* are in their faith journeys. For example, knowing how the concept of **Deserts** applies to the Christian life may help you better relate to a friend who seems stuck in his faith. Or an understanding of **Mountaintops** might help you understand someone who is struggling to describe a profound spiritual "high."

But whatever benefits this book's vocabulary lessons may offer us, we should continue our Christian walk bearing in mind James Martin's reminder of God's eagerness to accompany us all the way: "For every step you take toward God, God takes two steps toward you; and if you come to God walking, God comes to you running."[8]

---

[8] James Martin: Source unknown.

PART 1: The Journey's Basics

Sitting

Read Genesis 18

<u>*Key Verse*</u>: *"The* LORD *appeared to Abraham near the great trees of Mamre while he was sitting at the entrance to his tent in the heat of the day." (Verse 1)*

The idea of sitting or being seated conveys a host of meanings, ranging from resting to firmly instructing your dog to "sit!" Sitting can be either passive or active, a time to veg or a time to be engaged. For example, "I mowed the lawn, chopped a cord of wood and milked the cows. I just need to sit." Time to relax. Or the person interviewing you for the accounts payable job, who says, "Ah, yes, Ms. McCurdle, please be seated." No vegging here.

We encounter a comparable range of sitting/seated examples in Scripture. Think for example of the angels seated in Jesus' tomb (Jn. 20:12) and the various verses indicating that after Jesus' ascension He would be seated beside the Father.[9]

But our focus is on Abraham's experience in Genesis 18 and the recognition that sitting is good. It's certainly good to sit and rest in the heat of the day. Whatever work Abraham may have done that day was accomplished either early in the morning or lay ahead of him after the day cooled toward evening. But here he is, doing what he probably did each day, only to have his routine interrupted by three strangers. The rest of the chapter describes how he responds to the arrival of these mysterious strangers (one of whom is apparently the LORD Himself).

As is expected in the Middle East, Abraham gets up and welcomes the strangers and embraces the role of host by offering them something to drink. They have apparently been traveling in the heat of the day, odd though that may be, as most travelers would journey in the cooler times of the day. Abraham also provides water for washing their feet and then instructs Sarah to start preparing a generous meal.

There's much we can tease out of this chapter, such as the mysterious knowledge they display: How is it that they know Sarah's name? How can they promise that she will bear a son? Our concern here, however, is with the implications of Abraham's sitting—and that he stops sitting.

Sitting is a passive activity, physically. We may be sitting on the couch watching a Netflix production. Or sitting at our desk, working on our laptop, or making a phone call for work. But while our bodies are

---

[9] Mark 16:19 is but one example.

largely at rest, our minds may be fully engaged. We're immersed in our routines, whether we're just relaxing, or intensely engaged mentally. The lesson we learn from Abraham, however, is that he knew when to end his passivity and move into action. In this case, the need for action, and the form it should take, was plain. The Middle Eastern demands of hospitality, even before he knew he was about to encounter the LORD Himself, required that he shift gears from passivity into activity. In this instance, the trigger for displaying the hospitality he did was cultural. For us too, cultural expectations may show us the minimum of what God expects of our interactions with others. But that would be a bare minimum.

Think of the episode when Jesus goes to dinner at the home of Simon the Pharisee, who gets all huffy when the "sinful woman" washes Jesus' feet with her hair and her tears and anoints Him with precious perfume. The encounter climaxes with Jesus skewering Simon for his inaction:

> *Then he turned toward the woman and said to Simon, "Do you see this woman? I came into your house. You did not give me any water for my feet, but she wet my feet with her tears and wiped them with her hair. You did not give me a kiss, but this woman, from the time I entered, has not stopped kissing my feet. You did not put oil on my head, but she has poured perfume on my feet. Therefore, I tell you, her many sins have been forgiven — as her great love has shown. But whoever has been forgiven little loves little." (Lk. 7:44-47)*

Jesus uses this encounter primarily to speak to the question of forgiveness. Yet we can learn much from the woman, who didn't sit on her rear end but actively showed her love for and gratitude to Jesus. Similarly, Christians today ought to display our love and gratitude by moving from passivity to action when opportunities arise.

Another dimension to Abraham's hospitality is that he committed to hosting them *before* he knew their divine status. As the writer to the Hebrews put it, "Do not forget to show hospitality to strangers, for by so doing some people have shown hospitality to angels without knowing it." (Heb. 13:2) We too would be well advised to assume that any time we have been prompted to get out of our seats, we may well be participating in God's plans without knowing it. Like Abraham, we quite literally may not know what we are doing — or at least, not know the full scope of what we are doing. But we do know that there's been an intrusion in our lives. And that we can no longer stay seated.

Standing

Read Philippians 4:1-3

<u>Key Verse</u>: *"Therefore, my brothers and sisters, you whom I love and long for, my joy and crown, stand firm in the Lord…" (Verse 1)*

Consider:

- *Take a stand against crime.*
- *Stand up, stand up for Jesus!*
- *Don't stand on ceremony.*
- *Stand up and be counted.*
- *Stand someone up.*
- *Custer's last stand.*
- *The chairman had no choice but to stand down from his position.*
- *Please stand for the reading of the Gospel.*
- *I won't stand for that behavior.*

~~~~

If you're so inclined, spend a few minutes playing with this word and add as many other examples as you'd like. But even without adding your own examples, you'll see that "standing" is a versatile concept, and one that includes plenty of positive connotations for the Christian.

Let's begin with the verse from Philippians, cited above, "stand firm in the Lord." One could argue that this commitment to standing firmly in the Lord is foundational to any other kind of faith-related standing we might be engaged in. William Barclay says of the Greek word for "stand fast" that it is "used for a soldier standing fast in the shock of battle, with the enemy surging down upon him."[10] One crucial aspect of "standing" for the Christian is therefore to remain committed to our Lord no matter the pressures or threats we face. But if we find that a daunting prospect, Paul adds the wording, "in the Lord." Our potential for standing firm against whatever the battle may bring is grounded in the Lord Himself. We are neither expected, nor should we try, to take a stand for the Lord without Him. Elsewhere Paul warns us against complacency when he writes, "if you think you are standing firm, be careful that you don't fall!" (1 Cor. 10:12)

Up to now we have seen "standing" used in a general sense. But sometimes in Scripture we see God giving an explicit and direct command for

---

[10] William Barclay: *The Daily Study Bible: The Letters to the Philippians, Colossians and Thessalonians*, 71.

someone to stand or stand firm, right now. Paul's general counsel in Philippians echoes Moses' words when the children of Israel are about to cross the Red Sea, and the Egyptian army is getting terrifyingly close: "Moses answered the people, 'Do not be afraid. Stand firm and you will see the deliverance the LORD will bring you today. The Egyptians you see today you will never see again.'" (Ex. 14:13)

Here are three additional examples of context-specific commands to "stand."

- God tells Joshua to command the priests to stand in the Jordan: "Tell the priests who carry the ark of the covenant: 'When you reach the edge of the Jordan's waters, go and *stand* in the river.'" (Josh. 3:8)
- An angel approaches Daniel in a vision: "Daniel, you who are highly esteemed, consider carefully the words I am about to speak to you, and *stand up*, for I have now been sent to you." (Dan. 10:11)
- Jesus is about to heal the man with the shriveled hand: "*Stand up* in front of everyone.*" (Mk. 3:3)

~~~~~

We see in both usages (the general and the specific) that standing is active, not passive. Perhaps God calls us to action, to take a stand in a given situation, either literally (like the priests in the Jordan or the man with the shriveled hand) or in a symbolic or metaphorical way, as with Daniel. This type of standing requires a commitment, a willingness to trust God. This may be our initial commitment to Christ, when we first take a stand, as it were, for Jesus. That may come at an evangelistic rally or in response to an altar call in your church; or it may be in the quiet of your home one night, as you respond to the Holy Spirit's call. From then on, though, you are taking an ongoing, general stand for Christ and His Kingdom. Discipleship entails being an active participant in His plans.

Another implication of "stand" or "standing" in Scripture includes that of being on guard duty. An example of standing—and waiting and watching—comes from Habakkuk: "I will stand at my watch and station myself on the ramparts..." (Hab. 2:1) At times, nothing is expected of us but to be alert and attentive to our surroundings. Maybe we are awaiting word on what God would have us do next. But as we'll see in **Waiting**, standing can have the clear connotation of being primed for action. As Charles Spurgeon puts it, "'Stand still'—keep the posture of an upright man, ready for action, expecting further orders, cheerfully and patiently awaiting the directing voice, and it will not be long ere God shall say to you, as distinctly as Moses said it to the people of Israel, 'Go forward.'"[11]

~~~~~

---

[11] Quoted in *Streams in the Desert*, 132.

"O Lord, never suffer us to think that we can stand by ourselves, and not need thee."

– John Donne

Walking

Read Isaiah 30:19-21

<u>*Key Verse*</u>*:" Whether you turn to the right or to the left, your ears will hear a voice behind you, saying, 'This is the way; walk in it.'" (Verse 21)*

Notwithstanding the numerous other entries in this book that point to the "non-walking" phases on our journey, walking remains the preeminent way we move ahead in our Christian faith. Yes, at times we are **Sitting** or **Running**, or enjoying a **Mountaintop** experience. But most of the time we are walking.

Think of the marvelously inspirational passage in Isaiah which assures us that despite fatigue, we shall "mount up with wings like eagles." (Is. 40:31) *The Interpreter's Bible* comments on this passage as follows: "[T]he main company of God's people neither fly nor run: they *walk*. The largest part of the world's most useful work is accomplished by plodders." The writer continues: "Ministers in their parishes, teachers in Sunday schools, workers in missionary enterprises, scholars in the church's institutions of learning, who trudge along undiscouraged, year in and year out, are those upon whom men depend."[12] These are the faithful ones who walk.

It is no coincidence that Christians speaking about their faith do so in terms of our "Christian walk." Yes, the image is overworked. Yet it's such a useful picture that we Christians keep using it. Same with our role as "ambassadors for Christ," or "fighting the good fight" and "running the race." These biblically grounded images were rich when Christians first used them. Now, because the concepts they represent are central to our theology, we keep using these phrases because they remain effective shorthand for what we want to say.

"Walking" comes with various connotations, as we'll see in subsequent entries. We can be confident of three things, however:

- <u>For most of us, the journey will be varied and unpredictable</u>. At times on our journey we may find our walk interrupted by **Leaping** or **Limping**, **Soaring** or **Stumbling**. At times we'll encounter darkness and desert conditions. These may be offset by other encounters on **Mountaintops**, perhaps as a result of unexpectedly finding ourselves in **Thin Places**.
- <u>Our walk will always be under God's protection</u>, for we will

---

12 *The Interpreter's Bible*, vol. 5, 447. Emphasis in original.

always have God as our **Traveling Companion**. Here's what the writer of Proverbs tells us:

Listen, my son, accept what I say, and the years of your life will be many. I instruct you in the way of wisdom and lead you along straight paths. When you walk, your steps will not be hampered; when you run, you will not stumble. Hold on to instruction, do not let it go; guard it well, for it is your life. Do not set foot on the path of the wicked or walk in the way of evildoers." (Pr. 4:10-14)

This passage is particularly rich in the imagery of walking and running, coupled with an assurance of God's protection: "your steps will not be hampered" when walking, "you will not stumble" when running.

• <u>God is always ready to guide our steps</u>. As we saw above, Isaiah notes God's promise to the nation of Israel: "Whether you turn to the right or to the left, your ears will hear a voice behind you, saying, 'This is the way; walk in it.'" (Is. 30:31)

~~~~~

We in turn supplement His care and guidance, affirming that is how *we* choose to journey through this life. For the psalmist, the choice is clear: "I shall walk in the presence of the Lord..." (Ps. 116:9, *Revised English Bible*) And Isaiah urges the children of Israel, "Come, descendants of Jacob, let us walk in the light of the LORD." (Is. 2:5)

But let us give the last word to an Old Testament saint of whom we hear too little in our pulpits, the patriarch Enoch. He was the father of Methuselah, who is far better known. That's because Genesis says he lived longer than anyone else, 969 years. Another reason we tend not to hear much about Enoch is that preachers struggle to explain the mysterious end of his life. As Genesis puts it, "Enoch walked with God; then he was no more, because God took him away." (Gen. 5:24) Matthew Henry says Enoch was "the brightest star of the patriarchal age." He adds, "It is but little that is recorded concerning him; but this little is enough to make his name great..."[13]

What are we to make of the wording, "then he was no more"? How does that tie in with walking faithfully with God? The end of this man's faith journey is steeped in mystery. He is one of only two people in Scripture of whom it is said they did not die but entered God's presence directly. The other is the prophet Elijah. (2 Ki. 2:11) Unlike Elijah's departure, Enoch's end is described in the cryptic words, "then he was no more."

We are given clear justification for why Enoch was spared a natural

---

[13] Matthew Henry: *One-Volume Commentary on the Bible* 16.

death. It was because of his faithful walk with God. The writer to the Hebrews, in the important chapter commending the patriarchs for their faith, says: "By faith Enoch was taken from this life, so that he did not experience death: 'He could not be found, because God had taken him away.' For before he was taken, he was commended as one who pleased God." (Heb. 11:5) Echoing that view, the *New Bible Dictionary* says that "Enoch was a man of outstanding sanctity who enjoyed close fellowship with God."[14]

Let's take a closer look at what is meant by Enoch's "faithful walk" with God. The *New International Version* study notes point out that the wording "walked with God" replaces the word "lived" elsewhere in the Hebrews chapter. That "reminds us that there is a difference between walking with God and merely living."[15]

One commentator's reflection on Enoch's experience of "walking with God" merits quoting at length:

> To walk together with a human friend has clear meanings which have their reverent expansions in what it means to walk with God. It is to have the same goal and so to be moving in the same direction. It is to have the serene and happy sense of companionship upon the way. And it is to have unforced, spontaneous conversation as one goes along: sometimes to keep silence and just feel the other's presence, sometimes to speak out what is in one's mind and heart, sometimes to listen to what the greater Friend will tell us of the road, what to look for on it, and the goal to which we go.[16]

~~~~~

If we are seeking a role model for our faith journey, we needn't look further than this "star of the patriarchal age," whom we can easily imagine saying, "*This* is the way; walk in it."

---

[14] *New Bible Dictionary*, 2nd ed, 333.
[15] *New International Version*, study edition, 14.
[16] *The Interpreter's Bible*, vol. 1, 531.

Running

Read 1 Timothy 6:12

Key Verse: "Run your best in the race of faith…" (Verse 12, Good News Version)

Eric Liddell was one of Scotland's best. A gifted athlete, he represented his country in rugby and on the track. His deep faith, shaped by growing up in China as the son of missionary parents, led him to use his giftedness for God's glory. His story is splendidly, and mostly accurately, told in the 1981 film *Chariots of Fire.*

The film's climax concerns his participation in the 1924 Olympics in Paris, when he refuses to run in a heat for his best event, the 100 meters, because it is to be held on a Sunday. Despite intense pressure from the British Olympic officials, he withdraws from an event in which he is seen as a strong favorite for the gold.

Instead, he enters the 400-meters event. This is where the film deviates from the truth; the Sunday heat for the 100 wasn't a last-minute surprise for Liddell. He had in fact been practicing for the 400 after learning months earlier about the scheduling conflict. He goes on to win the gold with a world record time of 47.6 seconds. He subsequently returns to China as a missionary, following his parents' footsteps, where he dies in an internment camp run by the occupying Japanese in World War II, aged forty-three.

There's much to learn from this exemplary athlete and Christian, both from the film and what's been written about his life. Yet there's one moment early in the film that we will explore in **Stumbling and Falling**.

~~~~~

In several of his letters, Paul uses the image of Christians running a race. In Galatians he refers to the pitfalls that we can encounter: "You were running a good race. Who cut in on you to keep you from obeying the truth?" (Gal. 5:7) In other words, "Who tripped you? No matter, get up and keep running."

Paul would have been thrilled to see Eric Liddell in action, showing how his giftedness on the track and rugby field meshed perfectly with his Christian witness. Elsewhere, Paul speaks of winning the race, and that only one runner wins a prize. "Run in such a way," he adds, "as to get the prize." (1 Cor. 9:24) Of course, he's not speaking about a zero-sum game where there's only one winner and the rest of us are also-rans; he's speaking about the individual race in which we're each participating, and in which we need to endure to the finish line.

For running is hard work and training for a race is even harder. One of the scenes in *Chariots of Fire* shows Liddell and the other runners running on beach sand, a tough surface, to prepare them for the track where the race itself will occur. Hardened runners face all kinds of barriers, from shin splints to cramping. But as any three- or four-year-olds will show by the sheer pleasure on their faces, they have grown to the point where they can run with confidence — and even have a race with Dad (and wise dads know to lose, at least sometimes).

Running is not our default mode of movement, however. We are made for walking, as we've noted previously. But we can run for the sheer fun of it (think again of three- and four-year-olds in a park) or, as countless numbers of teens and adults do, run for exercise and overall fitness. Or we can run to escape harm, as we see in **Fleeing**, whether it's dashing to get inside during a heavy downpour or fleeing that grizzly bear that appeared out of nowhere on your hiking trail.

So too with our spiritual life. Most of the time we are walking; that's our default mode, spiritually as well as physically. At other times, though, we are in a sustained season of spiritual richness and growth. Perhaps it's during a college class on some aspect of theology or the Bible, or we are in a small group Bible study that's proving to be surprisingly enriching. Or maybe we're opening up a new and deeper chapter in our prayer life. Whatever it is, we know this won't last indefinitely, especially if we have had a mountaintop experience that ends with us returning to the valley. Sooner or later, we return to walking.

But a warning is in order here. When we're running, we are more vulnerable to **Stumbling and Falling**. We read in that reflection about Eric Liddell taking a tumble. Christians are especially vulnerable to temptation when they are "riding high." The *Africa Bible Commentary* refers to the sin of Achan, which was linked to the Israelites' defeat in the battle against Ai. (Josh. 7) This victory came soon after their miraculous defeat of Jericho. As a consequence of the tumbling down of the walls and the conquest of the city, "these men and women of God were perhaps too elated after Jericho to be spiritually alert. This is a very important lesson. It is often after a major victory that we are most vulnerable. It is at that moment when we think we have God on our side that we can easily become arrogant and proud."[17]

It is when we are running hardest that we are most prone to tripping. Many "high flying" pastors who have had successful ministries came crashing down after yielding to temptation, typically in the realms of money, sex or abuse of power. As these pastors and other Christians

---

[17] *Africa Bible Commentary*, 274.

learned, you hit the ground that much harder when you trip while running. God invites us to walk *and run* with Him and He is there to pick us up if we fall. But He would far rather we walk without stumbling than run and do a spiritual faceplant.

PART 2: Points of Interest, Warnings and Other Markers

Approaching

Read Hebrews 4:14-16

Key Verse: *"Let us then approach God's throne of grace with confidence, so that we may receive mercy and find grace to help us in our time of need." (Verse 16)*

For many Christians, Nehemiah is a much-admired biblical character. He is a Jew who grew up in exile and somehow became the cup bearer to the Persian king, Artaxerxes. Raymond Brown notes that "The wine steward was a man of recognized dignity in court circles, entirely trustworthy, the king's confidant and next in rank to princes."[18] When Nehemiah learns of the poor conditions in Jerusalem, his spiritual home, God instills in him the desire to use his high rank to do something about restoring the city.

So, after extended prayer, and a delay of more than a hundred days, he dares to bring up this concern when the king asks why he looks so unhappy. Not only is he saddened by the situation in Jerusalem, he has good reason to be apprehensive in raising this matter with the king. As Brown points out, "Nehemiah wanted to recommence the work the king had earlier forbidden. It was an immense undertaking and his first obstacle was reversing the king's orders."[19]

Not only does he ask the king to change his mind, but he also requests permission for a leave of absence and the resources to do the project. This is an astonishing example of biblical chutzpah, that wonderful Yiddish word meaning audacity or cheek. An example is a cartoon of a fellow in a bookstore who says to the clerk, "I want a book on chutzpah and I want you to pay for it."

Nehemiah persuades the king to let him undertake this major project, as described in the rest of the book: a story that provides one lesson after another in godly leadership. Our concern here, however, is with Nehemiah's approach to the king and how it compares with and differs from the Hebrews verse cited above.

Unlike Nehemiah, we have immediate access to our Lord. We need not spend a hundred days waiting for the right opportunity to enter God's presence. Also, we can do so "with confidence," as the writer to the Hebrews points out. While never trivializing or underestimating the

---

[18] Raymond Brown: *The Message of Nehemiah*, 41.
[19] Ibid, 41-42.

holiness of the One Whose presence we enter, we can approach Him knowing that we are infinitely beloved. If we turn to the image of the Lord's table, we know that we are always welcome guests. We must therefore approach His presence with a peculiar mix of solemnity, remembering God's holiness and sinless nature, and joy, as we remember that He is a God of infinite grace. The book of Isaiah provides a useful illustration. In chapter 6 we read how the prophet is overwhelmed by God's glory, to the point where he asserts, "I'm as good as dead!" (Is. 6:5, *The Message*)[20] Isaiah's awareness of his sinfulness in God's presence is summarily dealt with by the angels so that when the Lord says, "Whom shall I send? And who will go for us?" he responds, "Here am I. Send me!" (Is. 6:8) Note that he has no idea what the assignment is, or God's terms of service. He is so overawed by his spiritual renewal that he's ready to serve God however He chooses. The lesson for us? Approaching God, being in His presence, can have momentous consequences. We dare not approach Him lightly.

Think for a moment of a plane on approach to its landing in Atlanta. Without seeking to force the analogy, several parallels exist to the way we approach God. For one thing, both the plane and we are anticipated. The air traffic controllers at the Hartsfield-Jackson Atlanta airport are guiding the pilots, just as the Holy Spirit is drawing us into God's presence. And the pilots prepare for the approach, which demands full engagement with their situation as they use navigational aids and their instruments to make sure they're on the right flight path. No matter how hectic things get at this busiest airport in the country, with 2,700 planes arriving or departing daily, the Atlanta ATCs deal with each flight individually. Similarly, God deals with each of us, as individuals in countless numbers, as we approach Him. Our desire to be in God's presence—in prayer, meditation, or corporate worship—requires our equivalent of full engagement as we approach Him.

Let us return to Nehemiah, who explains to the king why he is unhappy. By contrast, we come before our King who already knows our every need and mood. Nor, as we seek to serve Him, will we encounter a need for our monarch to reverse any earlier decisions, unlike King Artaxerxes. That doesn't mean we come to our Lord with only timid requests. We ought to recall the words of Maltbie Babcock, who says: "[W]oe be to us if we are content with small service… Let us not be easily content… Our King deserves and expects kingliness."[21] We ought to be far more radical and imaginative in our anticipation of what God seeks to do through and for us, as Paul tells the Ephesians: "Now to him who is able

---

[20] The *New International Version* has "Woe is me!"
[21] Maltbie Babcock: *Thoughts for Every-Day Living*, 26.

to do immeasurably more than all we ask or imagine, according to his power that is at work within us…" (Eph. 3:20) Or, to put it differently, we should be living with a "holy audacity"[22]—a kind of "God-grounded chutzpah" that seeks even more than we can imagine.

Finally, the concept of "approach" by definition means one is approaching *something*. It can be King Artaxerxes, a runway in Atlanta, or a judge who tells the contesting lawyers to "approach the bench." Or the Lord our God, who never stops telling us, "Approach, any time. I'm expecting you."

~~~~~

Come near to God, and He will come near to you.

– James 4:8

---

[22] Quoted in *Streams in the Desert*, 107.

Baby Steps

Read 1 Cor. 3:1-3

<u>Key Verse</u>: *"I gave you milk, not solid food, for you were not yet ready for it. Indeed, you are still not ready." (Verse 2)*

Dave Ramsey is a syndicated radio talk show host who gives financial advice. He constantly advises his listeners to begin taking what he terms the seven "baby steps" toward financial health. The first is to "save $1,000 for your starter emergency fund;" the second is to "pay off all debt (except the house)."[23] One implication of his seven-step program is that one shouldn't attempt everything at once. Another is that simply getting started is crucial.

His approach is similar to that of the Japanese concept of kaizen, a philosophy meaning continuous improvement in which small steps, or baby steps, are taken toward a certain goal. If you look at toddlers, that's precisely what they are doing. First, they learn to crawl. Then, they pull themselves into an upright position, taking those first tentative steps— and falling down. But they don't give up. Instead, they get up and try again. Not much later they are running around the living room, increasingly aware of the gift of mobility into which they have grown.

It is the same with our spiritual lives. Maybe we grew up in a Christian home and have never known a time when we were not a Christian. Or perhaps we made a commitment to Christ as a teen or an adult. Either way, when this journey began it was marked by a basic, childlike spirituality. At this early stage our Bible knowledge was limited (most likely even for those coming to faith as adults, although not necessarily); our prayer lives were comparably simple. We had little grasp of theology. Instead of being able to digest a spiritual diet consisting of meat, we were still limited to milk. There's nothing wrong with a milk-only diet—if you're two months old. But not if you're five years old. Thus, we have Paul admonishing the Corinthian church for being spiritual babies: "I gave you milk, not solid food, for you were not yet ready for it. Indeed, you are still not ready." (1 Cor. 3:2)

Paul's goal is clear. He wants the Corinthian Christians, like Christians everywhere, to move toward spiritual maturity. Elsewhere he

---

[23] https://www.ramseysolutions.com/dave-ramsey-7-baby-steps#:~:text=Baby%20Step%205%3A%20Save%20for,pass%20Algebra%20II%20and%20Chemistry). Accessed May 20, 2024.

writes, "He [Jesus] is the one we proclaim, admonishing and teaching everyone with all wisdom, so that we may present everyone fully mature in Christ." (Col. 1:28)

A mature Christian walk would be the opposite of baby steps. What would the mature Christian look like? Stephen Rankin says, "Christian maturity ... entails specific dispositions and behaviors that show the disciple becoming increasingly like Jesus for the sake of accomplishing Christ's purposes in the world."[24] What then are the characteristics of Christians who have moved beyond baby steps?

- Their whole life is God-oriented.
- They are self-reflective about their faith.
- They can articulate the main aspects of their faith.
- They know where they stand theologically but are also open to change.
- They can live with paradox in their faith.
- They have a heightened awareness of their sinful nature, while at the same time...
- They have a heightened awareness of God's grace and love.
- They increasingly show the fruits of the Spirit in their lives, especially love.[25]

We don't move toward Christian maturity on our own. Presumably our parents encouraged us to move beyond the crawling and toddling stage, to when we could run, and then moved on to riding a bike, first with training wheels. Then with the flush of fear and excitement we went for our first ride without Mom or Dad holding onto us. So too with our faith journeys. We need others: our parents, Sunday School teachers, pastors, authors of faith-related books, and so on.

But if we're not moving steadily toward maturity, we merit the kind of kick in the spiritual rear that the writer to the Hebrews delivered to Christians who knew better: "... though by this time you ought to be teachers, you need someone to teach you the elementary truths of God's word all over again. You need milk, not solid food! Anyone who lives on milk, being still an infant, is not acquainted with the teaching about righteousness. But solid food is for the mature, who by constant use have trained themselves to distinguish good from evil."[26]

~~~~~

---

[24] Stephen Rankin: *Aiming at Maturity*, 6.
[25] This list is the author's own composite although it draws from Stephen Rankin's ideas. It should not be seen as definitive; you may identify other characteristics that you think should be added.
[26] Heb. 5:12-14.

Rankin says that "The Bible makes clear that God's telos [goal/aim/purpose] for believers is maturity—to become fully what God intends us to be."[27] So imagine God noticing a forty-year-old man who is crawling around the floor of his home. "Why aren't you walking?" God asks. "I know there's nothing wrong with you." The man replies, "Oh, I never got round to learning how." It's absurd to think that a physically able person would so willfully ignore his God-given potential. Then God says, "Now, about your spiritual development..."

---

[27] Stephen Ranking: *Aiming at Maturity*, 6.

Becalmed

Read John 3:5-8

<u>Key Verse:</u> *"The wind blows wherever it pleases. You hear its sound, but you cannot tell where it comes from or where it is going. So it is with everyone born of the Spirit." (Verse 8)*

Around the equator is a belt of often windless weather. That presents a problem for sailing ships, which could be stuck, immobilized for days or weeks. This belt is referred to as "the doldrums," a term that got applied to people who are apathetic, bored or listless. Or we could call it the blahs.

For Christians, this condition has the equivalent of a seemingly inactive Holy Spirit. Or at least, a Holy Spirit who blows where He pleases but these days apparently nowhere near me. I'm spiritually stuck. I'm in no danger of sinking. But I'm going nowhere.

The fact is, we know virtually nothing of God's activities in our world. We know what He is doing, at least to some extent, in our immediate environment. But much is going on behind the scenes, with God directing a play in which we have only the smallest roles. We are unaware of most of the other actors and the parts they play. That is perfectly fine. God neither needs nor wants us to know the entire script. Right now it may seem that our part has no speaking lines. We listen for the prompt off-stage, in case we've forgotten our cue. But no, there's nothing that the Spirit is calling us to contribute to God's drama right now, except our presence.

It's time for **Waiting**. And to mull over those deliciously paradoxical words of Reuben Welch, who says, "With God, even when nothing is happening, something is happening."[28]

---

[28] https://www.drjamesdobson.org/newsletters/dr-james-dobsons-august-2017-newsletter. Accessed May 7, 2024.

Big Steps

Read Joshua 1:1-6

Key Verses: "*After the death of Moses the servant of the* LORD, *the* LORD *said to Joshua son of Nun, Moses' aide:'Moses my servant is dead. Now then, you and all these people, get ready to cross the Jordan River into the land I am about to give to them….'" (Verses 1-2)*

Imagine you are poised to cross a Jordan River of your own. It could be getting married, taking a job in a new city, deciding where to go to college, or buying your first house. Whatever it is, it requires a major decision that will shape the rest of your life. The step, or steps, you take will parallel those of the priests who, at Joshua's command, stepped into the river to lead the Israelites across the Jordan. Notice though the conditions under which they did so: "Now the Jordan is at flood stage all during harvest." (Josh. 3:15) We're talking here about a river that's in flood, not a gently meandering stream. "Yet as soon as the priests who carried the ark reached the Jordan and their feet touched the water's edge, the water from upstream stopped flowing." (Josh. 3:15-16) Here we are witnessing priests who trusted that God knew what He was doing in requiring them to take that crucial first step. (Without, please note, life jackets or the presence of lifeguards.) Yet their high-risk behavior is exactly what God required of those men in that moment.

What about you? Your "crossing the Jordan" experience is unlikely to be accompanied by a dramatically visible miracle comparable to what these priests, and the nation they represented, encountered that day.

Most of the time our "Jordan crossings" are preceded by careful reflection and deliberate decision making. Few of us rush into marriage or decide to move across country on impulse. Instead, thoughtful Christians ground major decisions in accordance with what they believe God is telling them through Scripture and prayer. More often than not these decisions are also supplemented by consultation with friends and family, for affirmation of one's thinking.

Sometimes though, major decisions come upon us without time for careful consideration. When Joseph was commanded to take Mary and the Christ child to Egypt, he had no time to reflect on the angel's instruction; he had to move immediately. Given the clarity of his dream, he had no doubt about its authenticity as a message from God. If we are ever required to make a major decision but without comparable clarity, we can only trust the Holy Spirit to direct our thinking, perhaps supplemented by

37

a quick prayer for God's wisdom.

But whatever your circumstances, don't for a moment doubt that the God who is bringing you to the brink of your own Jordan experience knows exactly how to get you across. As Lynne Bundesen puts it, "[God] has not forgotten how to part the sea."[29] Or your Jordan.

---

[29] Lynne Bundesen: *One Prayer at a Time*, 9.

Bowing and Kneeling

Read Matthew 2:1-12.

<u>*Key Verse:*</u> *"On coming to the house, they saw the child with his mother Mary, and they **bow**ed down and worshiped him. Then they opened their treasures and presented him with gifts of gold, frankincense and myrrh." (Verse 11)*

If you're unfamiliar with Asian culture, you may be taken by surprise by the amount of bowing that takes place in the well received 2024 Hulu TV series titled "Shōgun." The series is based on the 1975 novel by the same title by James Clavell. Set in Japan in 1600, the story involves an English sailor who arrives in a politically divided Japan and gets caught up in the various leaders' machinations and scheming as they seek power. Initially, the Englishman is hesitant and tentative in how he goes about bowing as a sign of respect, not only to those of higher status but also as greetings to peers. But he soon learns the intricate body language of bowing.

In Western culture we generally find other ways to indicate our deference to our superiors. In the military, you will salute. When I was in school in South Africa, the class stood any time an adult entered the room. And there's the complex language of touch in Western culture. Think of a doctor tending to a patient in hospital. She finishes a conversation with a caring pat on the patient's shoulder. Or the coach sending a player onto the basketball court, with a pat on the back. In each case, it's the person of higher status or of greater power who initiates the touch. Young children haven't yet learned this unspoken rule and will with endearing spontaneity touch whomever they like.

Yet even though we don't observe the extensive protocols regarding bowing in Japan or other Asian cultures, Westerners still incorporate bowing into certain rituals. What to do if you happen to meet King Charles III of the United Kingdom, for example? The official royal website says "there are no obligatory codes of behavior—just courtesy. However, many people wish to observe the traditional forms of greeting. For men this is a neck bow (from the head only) whilst women do a small curtsy."[30] Why? To honor his role as monarch and show respect to him and his title.

---

[30] https://www.royal.uk/encyclopedia/greeting-the-king-and-queen#:~:text=The%20simple%20answer%20is%20that,hands%20in%20the%20usual%20way. Accessed May 7, 2024.

In his article titled "Bowing in the Service of God," Dr. Avital Hazony Levi writes from a Jewish perspective and says, "bowing is not an action unique to our relationship with God. In the Ancient Near East (and for much of history) people bowed before kings or any other powerful persons."[31] He continues, "[I]n bowing we come to understand the truth of the limitations of our power and knowledge. This new understanding shapes us to serve [God better]."[32]

Many Christians, especially those raised in Roman Catholic, Episcopalian or other liturgical traditions, incorporate into their worship some form of bowing. Perhaps on entering a pew, they may bow or curtsy toward the altar. During prayer, they may kneel, which is taking bowing a step further, so to speak. Officiants carrying out various roles in worship will pause and face the altar to bow when walking in front of the altar.

The Armenian Orthodox Church similarly takes bowing seriously. Fr. Barouyr Shernezian, for example, says that "the Armenian liturgy includes physical prayer practices as well. These physical practices help us encounter God with our bodies, as well as our spirits." He continues: "God gave Himself up as a sacrifice for our salvation. We should, therefore, bow down on our knees when we participate in worship. We should bring ourselves down to the ground and ask for His grace and mercy. We should bow down on our knees during the Divine Liturgy, as we participate in the sacrifice of God's Only Begotten Son, Jesus Christ."[33] Shernezian adds that bowing and kneeling are important exercises in humbling ourselves in God's presence—and in keeping with James' advice: "Humble yourselves before the Lord…"[34]

Bowing, whether from the neck or a full bow from the waist, and similar humbling gestures, like kneeling, benefit two parties: the person doing it, and the person to whom it is done. As we have seen, the bow is first of all to acknowledge someone deserving of honor. So we bow toward God, or a symbol representing God, like the altar. Or as the psalmist says, "I will bow down toward your holy temple…" (Ps. 138:2) The psalms contain numerous examples of bowing before God or something representing His presence, among them:

- "But I, by your great love, can come into your house; in reverence I bow down toward your holy temple." (Ps. 5:7)
- "Come, let us bow down in worship, let us kneel before the LORD

---

[31] https://hebraicthought.org/bowing-before-god-in-service/. Accessed May 7, 2024.

[32] Ibid.

[33] https://www.armenianorthodoxtheology.com/post/why-do-we-bow-down-on-our-knees. Accessed May 7, 2024.

[34] Ibid.

our Maker..." (Ps 95.6)

- "Exalt the LORD our God and bow down at his footstool. Holy is He." (Ps. 99:5, *Revised English Bible*)

But bowing brings benefits to us as well, including a conscious reassertion of our humble status before an almighty, holy God. We are reminded, especially if we adopt a posture of kneeling on either one or both knees, that we are dust and it is only by the grace of the God Whom we honor that we exist in the first place.

Shernezian offers an additional insight into the symbolism of bowing: "We bow down on our knees, putting our sins on the ground, and being raised anew by the grace of God. Every time that we bow, we remember Christ's burial and resurrection."

In many churches we witness another way we use our bodies to honor God, when we are invited to stand for the reading of the gospel. This act of **Standing** could easily be included in the reflection by that name, but more properly belongs here as our present focus is on how we use our bodies in a worship setting.

How do bowing and kneeling apply to your Christian journey and mine? They are, at least potentially, responses of respect or reverence that we demonstrate at certain times. It might be like visiting a cemetery, perhaps of military graves, where we pause momentarily before a grave or tombstone, standing silently in recognition of the life represented before us. We move to another grave and do the same. We are showing respect for these deceased individuals, whom we don't even know. How much more then, on our faith journey, should we take time to pause before God as we encounter one occasion after another that prompts a need to recognize His presence? We acknowledge that His presence demands a response of subservience and humility.

Those of us who are not accustomed to bowing or kneeling in church may find it awkward to start doing so now. We could, however, begin the practice of silently reciting a simple prayer whenever we take our seat in church. Maybe we could say the Jesus prayer: "Lord Jesus Christ, Son of God, be merciful to me, a sinner." Or we could make up one of our own. The point is to cultivate a habit of consciously recognizing we are in God's presence and that we grasp even in a limited measure the greatness of Who it is we serve.

~~~~~

The profound significance of a seemingly ordinary movement of our bodies, bending before something or someone greater than ourselves, was the culmination of the journey of the Magi. They knew on leaving their homes that they were drawn to greatness. Somehow, they knew on encountering the Christ child that they had found it. They gave Him their gifts and bowed down before a babe who would have no memory of the event. No matter. For this infant was to grow into the One of Whom Paul would one day write, "Therefore God exalted him to the highest place and gave him the name that is above every name, that at the name of Jesus every knee should bow…" (Phil. 2:9-10)

Checking the Map

Read Psalm 23:3

<u>*Key Verse:*</u> *He guides me along the right paths for his name's sake. (Verse 3)*

The South African writer Andre Brink recounted the possibly apocryphal story of a man known only as Corporal Martens, who lived near Cape Town in the late 1700s. Having had the chance to travel to the virtually unchartered interior, he drew a map of the country and sent it to the authorities in the hope of receiving some reward. Instead, he was warned that if he ever drew another he would get thirty years in prison. Apparently undeterred, Martins then secretly spent his days continuing his project.[35]

Unlike those colonial authorities who didn't want the corporal's map to fall into the wrong hands, God is only too eager that we follow His map for our lives. Let's turn to wikiHow for guidance on how to read a physical map (that is, a paper map).[36] The first guideline is that you need the right kind of map. Do you need one that tracks backwoods forest service roads that will help plan your hiking trip? Or do you need details on mileage on an Interstate highway so you can plan overnight stays?

Second, wikiHow advises you to properly orient your map; you want to be sure you're holding it so that north is up top. This way you can be confident of reading it correctly. Likewise, you need to understand the legend used for the map, showing railroads, highways, secondary roads, and so on. Also, it's important to know the scale used in the map.

Just as there are ways of reading a physical map, so too we should bring certain principles to reading God's map for our lives. What do God's map and "Christian map reading" look like? How are we to check God's map so that we can walk "along the right paths for his name's sake"?

We need to look at a combination of the five approaches to engage in what we could call "divine map-reading." In fact, God makes two maps available to us. The first indicates the big picture, like looking at a world map. In this map we see the God of history at work and His overall plan for humankind. But just as a map of planet earth isn't helpful for showing us how to get to an address in suburban Cleveland, neither does God's big-picture map give us specific guidance—for example, should I accept

---

[35] This anecdote is adapted from Gordon S. Jackson: *Breaking Story: The South African Press*, 216.

[36] https://www.wikihow.com/Read-a-Map. Accessed June 4, 2024.

the job in Tallahassee? That's where a much more granular look is needed. These days, most of us will consult our phones and Google will not only show us where to go but will also tell us of speed traps ahead and possible delays because of road construction or congestion. If conditions are bad enough, Google will even offer us an alternative route to save time.[37]

Imagine that we've reached a fork in the road on our spiritual journey or face an important choice as we look at our map. We're probably asking for trouble by proceeding on our trip without a check mark against each of these five lenses as we try to interpret our map.

1. These five lenses are not of equal importance. Scripture is a foundational and sufficient basis for the general principles of living a life devoted to the teaching of Christ; for the particulars of our daily lives we may need to supplement its directions with the other resources. More than any other avenue, however, God is likely to use Scripture to light our way. Especially when it comes to the general principles that should mark our lives, Scripture is a complete, coherent, and trustworthy guide. After showing us the general principles God wants us to follow, He gives us considerable freedom in making choices that are pleasing to Him.

At times God may speak to us in our specific situations through a particular Bible passage. Most often, though, we do Scripture an injustice if we expect detailed guidance from it. We wouldn't turn to the Sermon on the Mount for instructions on repairing a lawnmower. Likewise, we shouldn't demand detailed solutions from Scripture to our guidance needs that simply aren't there.

2. Next is prayer, which is also indispensable for discovering God's will and obtaining the wisdom and grace we need to live it out. Scripture offers us abundant guidance on God's general will for our lives and we don't need to spend much (or any) time in prayer figuring that out. Still, those seeking to follow Christ must turn to prayer for two needs: to discover God's particular direction for our journeys, and for the empowerment to undertake them.

Scripture is replete with encouragements for us to bring our needs before God, confident that He will both hear us and answer. For instance, Jesus gives us these familiar words: "Ask and it will be given to you; seek and you will find; knock and the door will be opened to you." (Mt. 7:7) And in John's gospel Jesus tells us, "But when he, the Spirit of truth, comes, he will guide you into all truth." (Jn. 16:13)

3. The third lens is the advice of mature Christians to affirm and confirm what we think God is telling us. Seeking advice from other

---

[37] As many of us have found, however, Google's directions (and those of similar programs) are not infallible. We ought not to follow them unquestioningly but bring our own judgment to what they tell us.

Christians on how to read our map is a sign of strength, not weakness. Proverbs says, "[W]isdom is found in those who take advice." (Pr. 13:10) The book of Proverbs is explicit about the need to seek out wise counselors who can steer us in a godly direction. For example, "The way of a fool seems right to him, but a wise man listens to advice." (Pr. 12:15) We're limited in our own knowledge and judgment, and others who care about us may stretch our perspectives on the options we face or point out pitfalls on the road ahead, potential problems we haven't considered. Route A may look appealing, but a Christian friend may have a good reason for you to consider Route B instead. Sometimes we are timid or unsure about pursuing a certain course and good advice can be as much an encouragement as it can be a confirmation we're on the right track.

4. While never the final word, circumstances can help us sort through the authentic and unreliable messages we may get in trying to interpret our map. If we were in a car with young children, it would be helpful to know that Route A has a rest stop in twenty miles, while there's nothing on Route B for another sixty. That circumstance will probably make us choose Route A. Likewise, spiritual choices always need to be responded to in some context—that of our education, our personal lives, our careers, our church lives, and so on. That context is made up of constantly changing circumstances that make a step we're considering possible or impossible, wise or unwise. The challenge we face is knowing how to "read" the road map of circumstances presented to us at any given time.

We can be sure that as we work our way through our map-reading process, our circumstances will eventually line up. Even though our circumstances may be the last piece of the process that falls into place, we can be confident that because God is sovereign over every aspect of our lives, He will make possible what He wants to happen to and for us.

Our circumstances are never to be taken as the final word in guidance; they must always be part of the overall process. Especially when we're dealing with major decisions, it's a good rule of thumb to ensure that our circumstances play a secondary role in guidance. They should confirm whatever else we've learned through Scripture, prayer, and our own judgment about the direction we should go. In other words, they should affirm, not dictate, what we understand to be God's leading.

5. The final consideration is a sense of inner peace. This isn't essential because by itself it's not a sufficient condition for choosing a course of action. Inner peace should be the culmination of the map-reading process. If we've worked our way carefully through each of the previous four steps, then this stage presents a final checkpoint. We're talking here about a sense of "rightness" of our decision or our choice "making sense" in the light of the Scripture reading and praying we've

done. Moreover, the decision or choice that lies ahead of us seems also to be compatible with both the advice we've received and the circumstances we face. If all of this is in place, then we come to the point where we ask, "Does all of this come together in a way that makes me confident God is wanting me to take Route A and not Route B?" Then we can trust the Holy Spirit to give us a sense of well-being and correctness about the next step — or, conversely, that the Holy Spirit will leave us unsettled or uncomfortable about going ahead if we ought not to.

Having a sense of inner peace about a decision is meaningless, though, if it stands by itself; without a "thumbs up" on the other four lenses (to mix our metaphors), feeling okay about a decision tells us nothing. Even if we've worked our way carefully through the entire spiritual map-reading process, this final lens is the least reliable of five. It is more subjective than the other four and is therefore more prone to being tainted by our wants and motives. Because of our limitations as sinful individuals, it's extremely difficult to know with absolute certainty that we're reading our map correctly. It's prudent, therefore, to be cautious in our reliance on our sense of inner peace about a choice or decision. Humility demands that, even if we feel assured we're on the right track, we move forward surrounding our decision in prayer that God will still stop us if we're about to take a wrong turn.

~~~~~

These lenses can assure us we're reading God's map accurately and that we're on the right road. It may be, however, as Max Anders says, that our map analogy isn't the best as we seek God's direction for our lives: "The Bible does not give us a road map for life, but it does give us a compass."[38] But whatever metaphor we find most helpful, we can be assured that God's maps are flawless and the compasses He distributes are utterly reliable.

---

[38] Max Anders: *Thirty Days to Understanding How to Live as a Christian*, 322.

Dancing

Read Psalm 149:1-5

<u>Key Verse</u>: *"Let them praise his name with dancing and make music to him with timbrel and harp." (Verse 3)*

Dancing has a mixed record in Scripture. Psalm 149 shows us the positive, joyful, exuberant side: this is an unhesitating call to praise Yahweh, in song and dance, together with the rest of His people, with timbrel and harp. You wonder if this psalm was either the occasion of quite a party or led to one. The New Zealand Bible scholar E. M. Blaiklock seeks to temper these holy high spirits, lest things get out of hand, by saying, "It is good to rejoice and be glad, but never without reverence, never without awe, never without some touch of the cross."[39]

When it comes to liturgical dancing in our churches today, many Christians are uncomfortable. While its proponents speak of the power to heighten the worship experience, Protestant congregations react with a mix of three responses: gratitude for something novel in Sunday's service; an awkwardness at not "getting" what's happening; and an entirely negative response to what is seen as a pointless, disruptive exercise devoid of any worshipful content.

Tempestt Spivey, then a senior at Rhode Island College, described in a 2020 interview for her college's magazine how she sees liturgical dance as a ministry. Her view is that "unlike other dance forms, liturgical dance isn't performed to entertain. It can be improvised or choreographed, and there is no particular liturgical dance style as you would find in other dance forms like jazz or ballet. 'Liturgical dance becomes whatever movements God gives the choreographer,' Spivey explained. It's spirit led."[40]

That's not how the Catholic church views the issue. In a 1975 document titled "Dance in the Liturgy," the Vatican came down squarely against the practice. While conceding that such dancing may have a legitimate place in some non-Western churches, it is unacceptable in the Mass. Why? In Western culture "dancing is tied with love, with diversion, with profaneness, with unbridling of the senses ... For that reason it cannot be introduced into liturgical celebrations of any kind whatever:

---

[39] E. M. Blaiklock: *Commentary on the Psalms*, 143.
[40] https://www.ric.edu/news-events/news/god-motion-sacred-art-liturgical-dance. Accessed May 8, 2024.

That would be to inject into the liturgy one of the most desacralized and desacralizing elements, and so it would be equivalent to creating an atmosphere of profaneness which would easily recall to those present and to the participants in the celebration worldly places and situations."[41]

Many conservative Protestants would resonate with the "profane" aspects of dancing, which traditionally was high on their taboo-conduct list, along with drinking alcohol, gambling and smoking. So strong was the cultural norm against dancing of any kind that it led to jokes like this. [Warning: Risqué joke ahead…] "Conservative Christians (or fill in your denomination of choice here) don't have sex standing up because it could lead to dancing."

These Christians can with good reason point to at least one biblical precedent where dancing didn't end well: the beheading of John the Baptist. When Salome performs what we can reasonably infer was a salacious, seductive dance before a beguiled King Herod, she asks for the prophet's head on a platter. (Mt. 14:6-12)

Another incident regarding dancing in Scripture involves David's triumphant return to Jerusalem with the Ark of the Covenant. "As the ark of the LORD was entering the City of David, Michal daughter of Saul watched from a window. And when she saw King David leaping and dancing before the LORD, she despised him in her heart." (2 Sam. 6:16) Commentators are unsure about the reason for Michal's reaction. One possible explanation is that his flamboyant behavior was beneath the dignity of Israel's king. Another is that his dancing and leaping revealed his underwear or even his private parts. It may also be that her strong reaction in fact had relatively little to do with David's dancing. Instead, she was angry for a host of other reasons: she was unable to have children; as Saul's daughter she was something of a political pawn and treated as such; and David may well have been a problem husband (think of his affair with Bathsheba). Taken together, seeing her husband so joyful while her life wasn't, may have been the trigger for a disproportionately negative response.

There's yet another aspect of dancing in Scripture that merits a brief mention. The memorable passage in Ecclesiastes that speaks of "a time to mourn and a time to dance," (Eccl. 3:14) clearly associates dancing with joy. The same emphasis comes in Jeremiah, where the LORD promises good to the children of Israel: "…go out to dance with the joyful." (Jer. 31:4) A few verses later we read, "Then young women will dance and be glad, young men and old as well. I will turn their mourning into gladness; I will give them comfort and joy instead of sorrow." (Jer. 31:13) Jesus

---

[41] https://www.catholic.com/qa/is-liturgical-dancing-permitted-at-mass. Accessed May 8, 2024.

includes in His parable of the prodigal son music and joyful dancing to celebrate his return. (Lk. 15:25)

~~~~~

It is noteworthy that all the biblical examples of dancing we've looked at are either communal dancing or occur in a public setting. Does that help us deduce what we are to make of our bodies' capacity for dancing? Perhaps the clue lies in the Catholic document quoted above and its reference to a difference between Western and non-Western views of dancing. When our favorite college basketball team clinches a place, in the last minute, in the Final Four, we may whoop and holler and give vigorous high-fives to anyone within reach. But we probably don't do a David-style dancing and leaping performance. We could. And depending on the level of excitement over that match-winning three-pointer, we may very well be jumping up and down. But it's hardly dancing. Nor does spontaneous dancing have a place in most Western churches.

There's no denying that social dancing brings great joy to many and that formal dancing like ballet requires great skill and artistry. There's no reason why Christians shouldn't be associated with ballet, for example. But dancing in general is subject to the simple question, "Is this dancing bringing honor to our Lord, or at the very least not undermining the cause of His Kingdom?" Would you be honored to have Jesus witnessing your dancing, or embarrassed? However you answer these questions, if you're not a dancing type at least consider what vehicle you would use instead to show others the joy that should mark your Christian journey.

Departing

Read Genesis 12:1-9

Key Verse: *"So Abram went, as the LORD had told him; and Lot went with him. Abram was seventy-five years old when he set out from Harran." (Verse 4)*

Departing can come in all kinds of forms. It can be voluntary, as when you retire from a job or move to a better one. Or less happily it can be a forced departure because you were fired. It can be a neutral statement of fact: "Our tour bus departs at 3 p.m. sharp; please be sure to be on board by then." Or it can be a more final, and euphemistic, kind of leaving: "There will be a viewing of the departed at Johnson's Funeral Home on Friday from 2 p.m."

Not surprisingly, then, we run into several kinds of departures in Scripture. One, like Abraham's, is a voluntary decision to leave home and head elsewhere, a profoundly important act of faith that ultimately leads to the birth of the nation of Israel, God's chosen people. Another example of this type is the departure of the children of Israel from Egypt. If the uncertainty associated with Abraham was his destination, the nature and length of the journey were the great unknowns for the Israelite nation.

A second type of departure entails someone else telling you, "Leave!" An example follows the miracle of Jesus directing the disciples who are fishing to cast their nets in deeper waters. The catch is so great that Peter is overawed by the gap between Jesus' power and his own sinful nature. "When Simon Peter saw this, he fell at Jesus' knees and said, 'Go away from me, Lord; I am a sinful man!'" (Lk. 5:8) We can be sure Jesus didn't take Peter literally and hasten away. He would have recognized Peter's remark for what it was: an exclamation of his own unworthiness, something Jesus already knew, long before this impetuous disciple himself departed from his commitment to his Lord by denying Him three times.

Yet another, and especially sobering, type of departure is when God Himself does the departing, abandoning a person or commanding someone to leave His presence. Take for example the encounter between the spirit of the dead Samuel whom Saul contacts via a medium. The prophet "said to Saul, 'Why have you disturbed me by bringing me up?' 'I am in great distress,' Saul said. 'The Philistines are fighting against me, and God has departed from me. He no longer answers me, either by prophets or by dreams.'" (1 Sam. 28:15) What a fearful realization had dawned upon Israel's first king. God had left him to his own devices, an inevitable outcome of his drifting away from Yahweh. By this stage, it seems safe to say, Saul had ended his walk with God.

~~~~~

Departing is an integral part of our Christian journey. We leave a job, we move from one town to another, we depart home for the first time to go to college. Sometimes these departures are painful, especially with the death of a loved one. Other times they are joyous, as when a young couple leave their respective families to marry.

More than many of the "movements" we make in life's journey, departures seem particularly fraught with emotion. For some of them, we can prepare, like our first (or last) child departing for college. Others take us by surprise. Yet in all of these changes, especially the tragic ones, we need to remain grounded in a faith that can equip us for the entire gamut of human emotions. Craig Barnes says, "One of my seminary teachers once cautioned that any theology that does not hold up in the emergency rooms of life must be held suspect."[42]

Then there's the matter of preparing for the inevitable: our final departure one day. John Baillie, a Scottish theologian, says of death that "Not even the most learned philosopher or theologian knows what it is going to be like. But there is one thing which the simplest Christian knows — he knows it is going to be all right."[43] For the Christian view of death entails comfort, hope, an assurance that God is in control, and the promise of eternal life.[44]

While we cannot begin to grasp what heaven will be like, C. S. Lewis may have put his finger on the essence of things. Imagining our response after death and arriving in heaven, he envisages us saying, "Of course! Of course!"[45] Far from it being a state in which we'll indulge in the kinds of enjoyments or pleasure we have known in this life, heaven will at the same time be both utterly familiar and radically different. It will not be a place of endless rounds of golf or fine dining. Instead, it will be as if for the second time we will have emerged from a womb into a life that was previously unimaginable. We can be sure that it will have all the hallmarks of the state of Shalom for which we strive in our current existence. As Thomas à Kempis wrote, "Wait for the promise of God, and you will have blessings in abundance in heaven."[46]

---

[42] Craig Barnes: *Yearning*, 23.

[43] Quoted in Gordon S. Jackson, *Grace for the Grieving: Words of Comfort in Times of Loss*, 10.

[44] This reflection is adapted from Gordon S. Jackson, *Grace for the Grieving: Words of Comfort in Times of Loss.*

[45] Quoted in Gordon S. Jackson, *Grace for the Grieving: Words of Comfort in Times of Loss*, 41.

[46] Thomas à Kempis, *The Imitation of Christ*, translated by Betty Knott, p. 135.

For when it comes to death, that final departure, we should be focusing less on that departure and more on our arrival.

Deserts[47]

Read Matthew 4:1

<u>Key Verse</u>: *"Then Jesus was led by the Spirit into the wilderness to be tempted by the devil. (Verse 1)*

Deserts have a special place in Scripture and Christians have long used them as a metaphor for their faith journeys. They convey a sense of isolation and hardship, where our senses are intensified and our capacity to hear God's voice is heightened.

Jesus began His ministry by spending forty days in the desert, clarifying His mission and resisting the most intense temptation to compromise what His Father had called Him to do. Nor was it a coincidence that He was following in the footsteps of Moses, who was forced to trade the luxury of Pharaoh's court for the harshness of the desert—the kind of territory through which, not coincidentally, he would later lead the children of Israel to the Promised Land. John the Baptist likewise located himself in the desert, living a harsh and spartan life, as he paved the way for Jesus' ministry.

Sometimes, as with John and Jesus, going to the desert is a voluntary matter. With Moses, he had little choice. On other occasions, "God brings us into a wilderness," says Matthew Henry, who adds, thankfully, "and there meets us."[48]

But regardless of what drives us there, deserts can be important places of instruction and preparation, incubators that strengthen us and prepare us for a task ahead. Their quietness and separation from the bustle of urban life allows us better to concentrate on God and hear His word to us.

A desert experience can be a bleak time, which we wish would end soon. On other occasions, God may send us into a figurative desert for a specific reason—or, a literal desert, as with Philip and his encounter with the Ethiopian eunuch. (Acts 8) Let us hear Matthew Henry again: "He [Philip] would never have thought of going thither, into a desert; small probability of finding work there! Yet thither he is sent. Sometimes God opens a door of opportunity to his ministers in places very unlikely."[49]

---

[47] This section is excerpted from Gordon S. Jackson, *Always Ready: A Christian Mandate*.
[48] Matthew Henry: *One-Volume Commentary on the Bible*, 32.
[49] Ibid, 1,667.

But a desert experience can also be a time of great enrichment, despite the discomfort or harshness associated with desert terrain. As Dennis Lennon wrote, "Whatever or wherever your 'desert' may be, it will be a place where our distorted minds are conformed, again and again, to the mind of Christ. It may be a solitary experience, or at times we may need the company of other Christians, with Bibles, books, pens and paper, for hard thinking and fervent prayer. That is the desert for you if it is the place of your mending."[50]

---

[50] Scripture Union *Daily Bread* Bible reading notes, no date.

Destination

Read Hebrews 11:1-12

<u>*Key Verse*</u>: *"By faith Abraham, when called to go to a place he would later receive as his inheritance, obeyed and went, even though he did not know where he was going." (Verse 8)*

~~~~~

"Grace tethers us to a place of knowing we belong to God and at the same time rolls us into uncharted waters."

— Mary Gray-Reeves[51]

~~~~~

It's odd. You're flying to Detroit this morning, but the boarding pass you got after checking your bag left the destination blank. You board your plane and the lead flight attendant tells the passengers, "Welcome aboard Flight 259. We know you have a choice of airlines so we appreciate your business. Please fasten your seatbelt and make sure your tray is secured and your seat is in the upright position." Yada yada yada. You've heard it all before. Then she says, "We're heading south but we don't yet know our destination."

"South? What do you mean we don't know our destination? What about Detroit?" Then the voices erupt. Someone says, "Hey, I thought I was going to Denver!" Someone else says, "I'm supposed to be going to New Orleans; what's going on?" A third voice says, "I want off; I want to know where I'm going."

Then the pilot's God-like voice comes through loud and clear. He says, "Good morning. I understand there's some concern about our destination. You should all know that when you commit to flying God-Air you leave the choice of destination to Me. Each of you is going somewhere I've chosen for you. Trust Me, I know what I'm doing." Then He adds, "Of course, if you're not comfortable with that, you're free to leave. But decide now; the cabin crew are about to close the doors so we can depart." Several passengers grab their hand luggage, jackets and briefcases, and hasten to the exit. You stay, confused but committed to this odd journey. A flight with no clear destination in mind? Unheard of. Yet if God is the pilot...

~~~~~

The online ***Merriam-Webster Dictionary*** says "A preposition is a

---

[51] Source unknown.

word — and almost always a very small, very common word — that shows direction (*to* in 'a letter to you'), location (*at* in 'at the door'), or time (*by* in 'by noon'), or that introduces an object (*of* in 'a basket of apples')."[52]

For our purposes, it's the bit about "shows direction" that's important. As we consider Abraham's readiness to obey the Lord's command to depart, we read that "By faith Abraham, when called to go to a place he would later receive as his inheritance, obeyed and went, even though he did not know where he was going." (Heb. 11:8) He was "called to go *to* a place," a place unknown. All he knows is the direction; he doesn't know the destination. Yet the calling he has received is compelling enough that he severs ties with Harran and leaving everything behind he heads into an unknown future, in an unknown place. God has indicated to him that "direction, not destination" is what matters.

On board that flight with the destination that God has in mind for you, you are in a sense flying blind, like the blind man we read about in John 9: "When Jesus healed the man blind from birth, he let him grope his way, still blind, to wash in the pool — and then the light broke. We don't need to know what we're groping toward — or why. It is enough that we have Christ's direction. The light will break in God's own time."[53]

So will clarity about the destination of Flight 259.

---

[52] https://www.merriam-webster.com/dictionary/preposition. Accessed May 8, 2024.
[53] Quoted in Gordon S. Jackson: *Quotes for the Journey, Wisdom for the Way*, 55.

Detours

Read Jonah 1:1-3

<u>Key Verse</u>: *"But Jonah ran away from the LORD and headed for Tarshish. He went down to Joppa, where he found a ship bound for that port. After paying the fare, he went aboard and sailed for Tarshish to flee from the LORD." (Verse 3)*

Jonah is the unsurpassed Old Testament example of someone who willfully takes a detour from what he knows to be God's direction for his life. He gets a clear call to go to Nineveh. Then comes the "but" that begins verse 3. That signals his brazen defiance and his decision to go to Tarshish, in exactly the opposite direction that God commanded him to go.

Jonah is hardly the only Bible character who succumbed to temptation and took a "spiritual detour." David commits adultery with Bathsheba, and then, after getting her pregnant, sends her husband to his death on the battlefield. Achan, who steals some of the spoil in battle against Jericho, causes the Israelites to lose the next battle, against the people of Ai. When he is found out, he loses his life and that of his family as well. (Joshua 7) All these people knew better; they all deviated from God's explicit directions.

In the New Testament the most shameful detour is Judas' betrayal of Jesus. So heinous is his action that his name is now a term of harsh condemnation. To call someone "a Judas" is a scathing insult. Other New Testament examples include Ananias and his wife Sapphira, who try to deceive the apostles by holding back some of the money from the property they sold, pretending they were giving it all to the young church. (Acts 5:1-10)

You will no doubt think of other examples. Yet others are identified in **Stumbling and Falling**, where similar sinful conduct is described. The difference is one of degree. Detours are calculated acts, in which we have ample time to reconsider our course of action. As Thomas à Kempis wrote, "…when temptation first appears, we must be especially alert, because it is easier to defeat the enemy if we do not allow him to set foot inside the door of the mind but meet him on the step as he knocks."[54] We ought to bar the door, yet like a Jonah or a King David we sometimes invite temptation inside and say, "Here, have a seat; make yourself comfortable."

The reflection on **Stumbling and Falling**, by contrast, focuses more

---

[54] Thomas à Kempis, *The Imitation of Christ*, translated by Betty Knott, 54.

on a sudden, unanticipated stumble rather than a carefully nurtured plan to do wrong. Biblical examples don't always indicate whether the person acted with premeditation or impulsively. Did Cain plan to kill his brother, or was that an impulsive act of rage? Same with Moses, and how he killed the Egyptian who was beating a Hebrew. In God's eyes, it doesn't matter whether our yielding to temptation was long nurtured or spontaneous.

While the precautions we can take will differ, the after-the-fact remedies are the same: "If we confess our sins, he is faithful and just and will forgive us our sins and purify us from all unrighteousness." (1 Jn. 1:9)

Equipped for the Journey[55]

Read Philippians 4:19
<u>*Key Verse:*</u> *"[M]y God shall supply all your needs according to his riches in glory by Christ Jesus." (Verse 19)*

Legendary Kenyan long-distance runner Eliud Kipchoge, the marathon gold medal winner at the 2016 and 2020 Olympics, also holds the world record, set in 2018. But it's his run the following year that interests us.

In October 2019 he became the first person to run a marathon in less than two hours. But the astonishing feat didn't merit world record status for a simple reason: it wasn't a real race. The event had been arranged specifically to see if he could break the iconic two-hour mark. A team of thirty-six runners pushed him to run an average of 4:33:5 minutes per mile—leaving him to cover the last 500 meters on his own. He finished twenty seconds under the two-hour mark. Two other factors helping him were a new type of Nike shoe that gave him an extra edge, and the carefully chosen flat course: the Prater Park, in Vienna, where the trees protected him from the wind.

The event was set up, in other words, not so much as a race but as a test: to see if he could break the two-hour barrier on a special course with every possible advantage. Therein lies a lesson for us. The writer of Hebrews tells us, "let us run with perseverance the race marked out for us." (Heb. 12:1) Like Kipchoge, we have a course marked out for us, set up by a God Who seeks to give us every possible advantage and resource. But so often we don't take advantage of what God seeks to make available to us. As God says through the prophet Malachi, "Test me … and see if I don't open up heaven itself to you and pour out blessings beyond your wildest dreams." (Mal. 3:10, *The Message*)

God knows our circumstances, strengths, weaknesses, and readiness to serve. In response, He tailors the course we are to run according to our individual needs. Your course may be similar to mine, but not identical. Or because of who you are, it may differ in significant ways. Regardless, God assures us of every advantage, beginning with the psalmist's assurance that those of us who seek to walk godly lives are "like a tree planted by streams of water." (Ps. 1:3)

---

[55] This reflection is adapted from Gordon S. Jackson: *Your Photo on God's Fridge Door.*

Having begun to mix our metaphors, with trees running the race God has set before us, let's add one more. Matthew Henry says, "God knows what He designs for us, that we be furnished with grace sufficient. He that appoints what the voyage shall be will victual [supply] the ship accordingly."[56] However we see our journey, then, by land or sea, we can be assured that we have a God Who is passionately seeking our success in the race marked out for us.

Alexander MacLaren says, "Each of us may be sure that if God sends us on stony paths he will provide us with strong shoes, and he will not send us out on any journey for which he does not equip us well."[57]

Equipping us for the journey and clearing the pathway does not mean an obstacle-free life, however. God is not a "curlingfiorde parent," a wonderful Danish term relying on the image, from the sport of curling, of a parent who scurries ahead of a child to smooth away every possible obstacle. The New Testament is rife with references to the difficulties we must expect in life, including at times even the possibility of suffering for our faith.

Nor are we given a Google Maps set of directions, with a roadmap accompanied by specific directions to move into the right lane and turn onto Broadway Avenue in 500 feet. But we can be assured that our equivalent of Eliud Kipchoge's carefully chosen course in Vienna is optimally designed for us. Nobody said running that course would be easy. Like running a regular marathon, for that matter, and suitably equipped with the right shoes.

~~~~~

"They [the prophets] declare your commands, but you give power to obey. They point out the road, but you give strength for the journey."

— Thomas à Kempis[58]

---

[56] Matthew Henry: *One Volume Commentary on the Bible*, 391.
[57] Quoted in *Streams in the Desert*, 37.
[58] Thomas à Kempis: *The Imitation of Christ*, translation by Betty I, Knott, 110.

Fences Misplaced

Read Galatians 1:6-9
Key Verse: "*Evidently some people are throwing you into confusion and are trying to pervert the gospel of Christ.*" *(Verse 7)*

Joseph Bayly once described an analogy about a community that lived on a high mesa, which had steep cliffs on all sides. As a precaution, the community's leaders fenced in their living space, so that no children would stray to the mesa's edge and fall to their death. The fences were essential to the community's safety.

Using this analogy in the mid-1900s to describe the "fences" that the US evangelical community erected to protect their values, Bayly lamented that they made the mistake of erecting needless cultural and moral fences. He cited the example of how movie-going or mixed marriages were seen as taboos in more conservative churches. Yet there was no biblical basis for such prohibitions.[59]

The problem, to return to the image of the mesa, was that incorrectly placed fences lulled people into a false sense of security. When people crossed them, and found that they didn't plummet to their death, they incorrectly concluded all the other fences could be ignored too. Which, of course, they couldn't.

While Bayly's target was his fellow evangelicals, the lesson applies to Christians of all stripes. We need to be wise in telling our young people in particular what the real faith-related dangers are that they face. We need good judgment in seeking balance. Setting up needless fences will inevitably breed cynicism about the value of *all* fences and people will disregard them. Setting up too few or even no fences, on the other hand, will lead to an "anything goes" approach, reflecting a church culture that accepts everything and thus stands for nothing. All of which calls for good theology to determine what God would see us have as "the right" fences. That warrants looking at a case study of a badly placed fence that ended up being moved for the right reason.

In late summer 2019, the owner of an event center in Booneville, MS, turned away an interracial couple wanting to get married. When the groom's sister followed up and asked her why she wouldn't host the

---

[59] Joseph Bayly: *Out of My Mind*, 114-116.

event, the white owner said, "We don't do gay weddings or mixed race."[60]

Asked why not, the woman added, "Because of our Christian race, I mean our Christian beliefs." The groom's sister asked her what passage in the Bible informed her beliefs, the owner said, "I don't want to argue my faith."

The City of Booneville issued a statement that condemned this discriminatory conduct. Then the story took an unexpected turn.

The event center's owner spoke to her pastor, after which she posted an apology on Facebook saying she was wrong; the pastor had shown her that nothing in Scripture prohibited interracial marriages. In part, her post said, "I truly apologize to you for my ignorance in not knowing the truth about this. My intent was never of racism, [sic] but to stand firm on what I 'assumed' was right concerning marriage." According to the BBC report of this story, the bride forgave the woman, who invited them to use the space.

The story's headline read, "Mississippi wedding venue refuses interracial pair over owner's Christian faith." That was accurate. But it was also incomplete. For part two of the story noted three steps:

- The woman questioned her theology.
- She sought help in clarifying her thinking, and consulted her pastor, and
- As a result, she changed her theological outlook—and behavior.

That's a three-step pattern all of us ought to follow as we look at the fences we think God has ordained for our safety. Steeped as we are in the Christian sub-cultures in which we have been raised or currently live, we need to work at distinguishing between the fences that are truly God-ordained and those that are artificial barriers our fellow Christians have erected—no doubt well-intentioned but misguided nonetheless. We need to be alert therefore both to misplaced fences, like the one about racially mixed marriages, and absent ones, such as when churches fail to address genuine issues of racial discrimination.

Even those of us who are professional theologians barely begin to grasp the nature of God and how He expects us to live. The rest of us most likely have an understanding of God that is even less complete. In other words, each of us should always be refining our theological thinking as we grow in our understanding of God. Like this initially misguided woman in our story, we need outside resources to nurture that growth: sermons, Bible studies, individual devotions and reading, conversations with Christian friends.

---

[60] https://www.bbc.com/news/world-us-canada-49571207. Accessed May 14, 2024.

An improved grasp of what God expects of us may necessitate a change in behavior, as this woman saw was needed. In her situation it required repentance and an apology, which to her credit she delivered. The story's headline, then, was incomplete: it failed to reflect the change in this woman's outlook—thanks to her willingness to question her theology, seek help, and act in response to a fuller understanding of Scripture's view of race relations, not the culture in which she had been raised. Not a bad way to deal with bad fences.

The Final Stretch[61]

Read Philippians 1:3-6

<u>Key Verse</u>: *"... he who began a good work in you will carry it on to completion until the day of Christ Jesus." (Verse 6)*

Let us return for a moment to Eric Liddell. We first met him in the reflection on **Running**, in Part 1. If you haven't yet read it, please do so now. We'll wait... (Good, you're back...)

Here's one more thought about that famous 400-meter race, which *The Guardian* newspaper in 2012 listed as one of the most stunning moments in Olympics history.

Asked beforehand what his strategy was for running this distance, Liddell said: "I run the first 200 meters as hard as I can. Then, for the second 200 meters, with God's help, I run harder."[62]

How can one run "harder than you can"? The answer lies in the phrase, "with God's help." It's reflective of Liddell's faith that he counted on God to help him do even better than his best, to do what was, in a sense, humanly impossible. Like Peter walking on water.[63] In response to Jesus' invitation to come and join Him on the water, Peter steps out of the boat and walks toward his Savior. He finds himself doing the impossible. Yet as Jesus told His disciples in their conversation about how difficult it was for rich people to enter the kingdom of heaven, "With man this is impossible, but with God all things are possible." (Mt. 19:26)

And Eric Liddell, with God's help, did the seemingly impossible that day at the Paris Olympics, running that second 200-meter stretch harder than he could in his own strength. Unlike poor Peter, who couldn't even make it a fraction of that distance when he took his eyes off Jesus.

In his epistle to the Philippians Paul speaks of his confidence "...that he who began a good work in you will carry it on to completion until the day of Christ Jesus." (Phil. 1:6)

God undoubtedly wants you to return home being able to say, "Mission accomplished." Not "Mission mostly accomplished."

---

[61] This reflection is adapted from Gordon S. Jackson: *Ninety Days of Difference*.
[62] https://www.theguardian.com/sport/2012/jan/04/50-stunning-olympic-moments-eric-liddell. Accessed May 18, 2024.
[63] Mt. 14:29.

Fleeing

*Read **1 Kings 19:1-9***

<u>*Key Verse*</u>*: "Elijah was afraid and ran for his life. When he came to Beersheba in Judah, he left his servant there, while he himself went a day's journey into the wilderness." (Verse 3-4)*

We never want to encounter a situation where we're forced to make a choice between "fight or flight." But despite the promise of God's protection, it may be that on rare occasions we'll need to make such a choice. We wouldn't be the first of God's people required to do so. In this reflection we'll look briefly at several biblical fight-or-flight situations.

We begin with Elijah. Fresh from his dramatic victory over the prophets of Baal and their subsequent slaughter, he faces the fury of Ahab the king and Jezebel his wife. (1 Ki. 18) He fears for his life and escapes into the desert. Elijah offers us an excellent example of one of God's people who felt compelled to flee to safety.

Fleeing is like **Departing**, but on steroids. Fleeing is not only leaving a situation, but doing so hurriedly, as fast as possible to escape an imminent physical danger or some other threat. We have already referred to Jonah in the reflection on **Detours**, which describes his deliberate deviation from what he knows to be God's will. Yet Jonah is a strong candidate for inclusion here as well. He detests the idea of preaching to the Ninevites and takes the first ship available in the opposite direction. (Jon. 1)

Next, we turn to Jeremiah 42. It provides an account of those Jews remaining in Judah after the Chaldeans have sacked Jerusalem and taken many of the land's inhabitants to Babylon as captives. Jeremiah is approached by the Jews making up this remnant who ask him to seek God's word on whether they should stay or flee to the presumed safety of Egypt. While they don't seem to face the same urgency as Elijah and Jonah, they are looking over the horizon and fear for their future, if not their very lives. Jeremiah returns to them ten days later and says God's instruction is for them to remain where they are. "Do not be afraid of the King of Babylon, whom you now fear," Jeremiah tells them. He underscores God's assurance and adds: "Do not be afraid of him, declares the LORD, for I am with you and will save you and deliver you from his hands." (Jer. 42:11) The remnant don't believe Jeremiah or his word from God. They angrily denounce the prophet and opt to leave for Egypt in defiance of God's promise of safety. It doesn't end well for them, in keeping with Jeremiah's verdict: "[Y]ou have not obeyed the LORD your God in what he sent me to tell you. So now be sure of this: you will die by sword, famine, and pestilence in the place where you want to go and live." (Jer. 42:21, *Revised English Bible*) Two chapters later we learn that the LORD recalls this warning and none of the remnant return to Judah. He has Jeremiah say, "[T]hey will not return; not one of them will survive, not one escape." (Jer. 44:14, *Revised English Bible*) This group of Israelites fled when they shouldn't have and paid the price for their willful disobedience. The most sobering lesson is to be learned from those fearful Jews who pretended to call upon God's help yet angrily disregarded it when the prophet told them what they didn't want to hear.

Nehemiah offers us a contrasting response to the self-deception and lack of integrity of the group who disregarded Jeremiah's prophecy. Facing intense opposition as he sets about rebuilding Jerusalem's walls, he says: "Should a man like me run away?" (Neh. 6:11) Given his clarity of purpose he chooses to stay and counter the opposition, having no doubt that he is doing God's work.

Let's shift to the New Testament, and the example of Joseph, who is charged with protecting the Christ child. His situation was unusual in that he didn't even know of the threat facing the infant Jesus. Fortunately, Joseph got perfect clarity in the form of an angelic message: "Leave, *now*." We have no details about the dream or anything about the angel. But we know that Joseph had no doubt whatever about the dream's authenticity. We know too that what he faced wasn't truly a fight-or-flight situation. There was no way he could take on Herod's forces bent on killing Jesus. Consequently, the infant Jesus is scooped up and hustled away by night to Egypt. Ironically, the baby Jesus is taken for safety to the land from which Moses led the enslaved children of Israel to freedom in the Promised Land.[64]

How does Joseph's experience speak to the fight-or-flight situations we might encounter? We must recognize that such difficult choices are usually a conflict between two values: the tenacity required to stay in a difficult, even dangerous, situation (not knowing how God may work things out), or the prudence that says, "cut your losses" and leave.

Unlike Joseph, we probably won't get such a clear divine direction on what to do next. That means we'll most likely have to use our God-given judgment to decide our next steps—a decision supplemented by prayer, a reliance on whatever guidelines we can identify in Scripture, and

---

[64] At this time there would have been sizeable Jewish communities in Egypt, especially in the coastal city of Alexandria. It is reasonable to assume that Joseph, Mary and Jesus found sanctuary in one of these communities. See for example William Barclay: *The Daily Study Bible: Matthew, vol. 1*, 24.

perhaps the advice of mature Christian friends. This is assuming of course that we have enough time to reflect on our fight-or-flight options. If we face a crisis that demands an immediate response, all we can do is use our best judgment and trust in God's protecting hand over us and our situation.

We can be sure that if we are ever in a fight-or-flight situation, and we genuinely seek God's direction, it may come in some miraculous form like a dream (unlikely though that is), or more probably through exercising our God-given common sense. The worst possible response, however, is to call upon God for His direction only to reject it when it comes.

So what is it to be, in our situation? Are we to flee or stay and fight? There's no easy answer. But if we choose to flee the equivalent of any Chaldeans in our lives, we need to recall that we cannot outrun or flee from God. Francis Thompson's famous poem, "The Hound of Heaven," begins:

I fled Him, down the nights and down the days;
I fled Him, down the arches of the years;
I fled Him, down the labyrinthine ways
Of my own mind; and in the mist of tears...

The poem ends with the recognition that he cannot outrun a God whose love will seek him relentlessly. Indeed, attempting to flee God is the ultimate folly. As the psalmist says, "Where can I go from your Spirit? Where can I flee from your presence?" (Ps. 139:7)

Following

Read Matthew 4:18-22

<u>Key Verses</u>: *"As Jesus was walking beside the Sea of Galilee, he saw two brothers, Simon called Peter and his brother Andrew. They were casting a net into the lake, for they were fishermen. 'Come, follow me,' Jesus said, 'and I will send you out to fish for people.' At once they left their nets and followed him. Going on from there, he saw two other brothers, James son of Zebedee and his brother John. They were in a boat with their father Zebedee, preparing their nets. Jesus called them, and immediately they left the boat and their father and followed him."* (Verses 18-22)

Indeed.com is the largest Internet job site in the world, claiming to have more than 350 million unique visitors to the site every month. In addition to playing matchmaker for job seekers and employers, the site hosts a number of useful articles on job-related topics. One of them is titled "What is Followership?" The article says, "While it's true that an organization is only as good as its leaders, it is also only as good as its followers."[65]

The article identifies fourteen attributes of a good follower. Most apply to the corporate world and to organizations. But several apply directly to what we could call Christian "followership," or more appropriately, "discipleship." Among these are:

- Ego Management
- Loyalty
- Humility and
- Work Ethic.[66]

The verses cited above include Jesus' famous invitation to "Follow me." To what end? To "make you fishers of men," as the well-known wording of the *King James Version* has it. Simon and Andrew are the first to sign up. Next are the sons of Zebedee, James and John, who likewise give up their livelihood to become Jesus' followers. They, along with eight other men, begin the arduous task of learning the ego management, loyalty, humility and work ethic (or total commitment) that Jesus demands.

---

[65] https://www.indeed.com/career-advice/career-development/followership. Accessed May 24, 2024.
[66] Ibid.

They had begun a journey of total commitment, one that Dietrich Bonhoeffer described in sobering terms: "When Christ calls a man, he bids him come and die."[67] According to what we know of early church history, many of The Twelve did in fact suffer a martyr's death. Jesus never hesitated to tell those who were considering becoming His followers two things: the cost of becoming a disciple, and the rewards. Both are described in the parables of the treasure hidden in a field and a pearl of great value:

> *The kingdom of heaven is like treasure hidden in a field. When a man found it, he hid it again, and then in his joy went and sold all he had and bought that field. Again, the kingdom of heaven is like a merchant looking for fine pearls. When he found one of great value, he went away and sold everything he had and bought it. (Mt. 13:44-46)*

Note the wording, "sold all he had" and "sold everything he had." This was the level of commitment that Jesus demanded of His followers. But note too what each of these men received: for one, it was great treasure that led to his joy, and for the other, the acquisition of a pearl so splendid and rare that it was worth liquidating all that he owned to buy it.

Not everyone is that eager to embrace the Kingdom of God that Jesus proclaimed, as we find in this account in Luke, which is worth quoting in full:

> *As they were walking along the road, a man said to him, "I will follow you wherever you go." Jesus replied, "Foxes have dens and birds have nests, but the Son of Man has no place to lay his head." He said to another man, "Follow me." But he replied, "Lord, first let me go and bury my father." Jesus said to him, "Let the dead bury their own dead, but you go and proclaim the kingdom of God." Still another said, "I will follow you, Lord; but first let me go back and say goodbye to my family." Jesus replied, "No one who puts a hand to the plow and looks back is fit for service in the kingdom of God." (Lk. 9:57-62)*

Here we meet three aspiring disciples who wanted to follow Jesus, but on their terms. The first hadn't taken into account the potentially itinerant, unsettled life that discipleship might entail. The second was ready to follow—but not yet. His father may have been elderly or ill (or both), and close to death. Maybe he was anticipating his inheritance. Or to be more charitable, perhaps he knew it would fall to him to sort out the estate and he felt obliged to honor that obligation. Alternatively, his father may have been in excellent health and the man's hesitation in following Jesus revealed he wasn't unequivocally committed to the kind of

---

[67] Quoted in Gordon S. Jackson: *Quotes for the Journey, Wisdom for the Way*, 41.

discipleship Jesus demanded. Whatever the man's reasoning, Jesus dismisses it out of hand. The third person's excuse seems reasonable. Why not go and say goodbye to one's family? Yet here Jesus is saying that committing yourself to following Me requires that you must make that your highest priority, even over family. As *The Interpreter's Bible* puts it, "None of them apparently is capable of the passionate loyalty to the kingdom of God which is required..."[68]

Then, sadly, there were those who started following Jesus but faded away. We encounter them in parable form, in Jesus' story of the sower and the seed. (Mt. 13) We meet them in person, however, in John's gospel. He records how for some disciples Jesus' teaching proved too difficult. As a result, "From this time many of his disciples turned back and no longer followed him." (Jn. 6:66) For one reason or another, they couldn't accept that Jesus required of them when "... he said to them all: 'Whoever wants to be my disciple must deny themselves and take up their cross daily and follow me.'" (Lk. 9:23)

~~~~~

The presence of followers presupposes there exists someone who is being followed. In other words, a leader. As civil rights leader Benjamin Hooks put it, "If you think you are leading and turn around to see no one following, then you are just taking a walk."[69] For more than 2,000 years, however, the Man from Galilee has inexplicably been a divine magnet. The Holy Spirit has drawn countless men, women and children into Jesus' orbit, as they embrace His claim to be God incarnate and a Savior for Whom they are willing to take up their cross daily. And follow Him.

---

[68] *The Interpreter's Bible*, vol. 8, 183.
[69] https://www.azquotes.com/author/24409-Benjamin_Hooks. Accessed May 24, 2024.

Getting Up

Read Mark 5:21-43

<u>*Key Verse*</u>: *"He took her by the hand and said to her, 'Talitha koum!' (which means 'Little girl, I say to you, get up!")." (Verse 41)*

Only the most pompous among us would tell our sleeping teenager, "Arise! School awaits." We ordinary mortals would no doubt say, "Get up; you'll be late for school." We would have plenty of biblical precedents for the first part of our admonition; Scripture is replete with examples of God or others telling people to "get up." (However, you'd search in vain for the "you'll-be-late-for-school" bit.)

We don't know if Jairus' daughter was late for school or not. We do know, however, that she wasn't yet a teenager. Mark's gospel tells us she was twelve. And that she had died. Mark's account leaves us in no doubt of her death. Jairus gets the message while he's been anxiously waiting for Jesus to finish ministering to the woman with the hemorrhage, as he fears life is slipping away from his beloved child. By the time that he and Jesus (and Peter, James and John) arrive at the house, the mourners are already at work, wailing away. When Jesus tells them the young girl isn't dead but only sleeping, they laugh at Him. But they have no idea Who they are dealing with, or the divine power He will soon bring to bear on this family tragedy.

Next, Jesus takes this dead child by the hand and tells her to "get up." Let's pause for a moment to reflect on the ramifications of what Jesus says. Telling a groggy teenager to "get up" is one thing. Telling a child, or anyone, who is dead is — on the face of it — absurd, foolish or self-deluding. Or even unbelievably cruel to the parents, who have only begun to accept that their child has died.

Yet that is precisely what Jesus says: "get up." And she does.

~~~~~

This young girl, whose name we don't know, is one of a select group of Bible characters who are told to "get up." As we look at a few others, we can draw some implications of what this succinct instruction implies. In the case of Jairus' daughter, it is "getting up" to a life restored. It is noteworthy that Jesus uses the same language in the town of Nain, where He raises to life the only son of a widow: "Then he went up and touched the bier they were carrying him on, and the bearers stood still. He said, 'Young man, I say to you, get up!'" (Lk. 7:14)

These two miracles primarily benefit the daughter and the son whose lives are restored. But they also are of enormous benefit to their families: the young girl's anguished parents and the widow, whose only means of support has now been given back to her.[70]

In these two instances, and that of Lazarus, premature deaths are reversed. The recipients of these miracles can now resume their lives, lives changed forever with the awe-inspiring realization that "I got to die and came back to life, thanks to a rabbi who commanded me to 'get up' and overrode the grip of death."

We also find references to "get up" commanded of God's servants whom He has selected for a particular task. Examples include that of Joseph, Mary's husband and guardian of the infant Jesus. As we see in the reflection on **Flee**, Joseph is told in a dream to escape to Egypt. "[A]n angel of the Lord appeared to Joseph in a dream. 'Get up,' he said, "take the child and his mother and escape to Egypt." (Mt. 2:13)

In the Old Testament we learn that Elijah gets a similar instruction. After fleeing for his life from King Ahab and his murderous wife Jezebel, he is exhausted and in hiding. That's when God sends help: "The angel of the LORD came back a second time and touched him and said, "Get up and eat, for the journey is too much for you." (1 Ki. 19:7)

Then, also from the Old Testament, there's God's instruction to Gideon in dealing with the Midianite army: "During that night the LORD said to Gideon, 'Get up, go down against the camp, because I am going to give it into your hands.'" (Judg. 7:9)

~~~~~

The phrase "get up" occurs eighty-one times in the *New International Version*. The close synonym, "arise," appears forty-one times. Not all of these uses are by God, Jesus or angels. But many are. In Mark's account of the healing of the blind man, we hear the crowd, not Jesus, telling him to "arise" or "get up," as many translations have it. (Mk. 10:49)

That teenager who needs to get up first needs to wake up. Time to introduce Jennie Litvack. She played the shofar, the ram's horn that's integral to Jewish worship. It is an instrument that goes back to biblical times. When she died in 2019, *The Economist* magazine wrote an obituary, paying tribute to her musical gifts. Like a military trumpeter, the shofar player has a number of different calls or signals, each conveying a distinct message. One played on the shofar is the *teruah*, "the nine staccato notes that, like an alarm clock, she would say, [that] would summon the listener,

---

[70] A parallel is found in Lazarus' resurrection, in which Jesus not only gives him back his life but also provides unimaginable comfort to his sisters Mary and Martha, as recounted in John 11. In this case though Jesus instructs the dead man to "come out," (verse 43) — not quite the same as "get up," but words having the same effect.

'Wake up, wake up, wake up. Now is the time to do something.'"[71]

Every now and then we need the *teruah* to break into our routines, with its call, "Wake up, wake up, wake up—now is the time to do something." It may be that today God will tap you on the shoulder, or if necessary, shaking you awake, and saying, "Get up, I have work for you."

---

[71] *The Economist*, July 19, 2019.

Go!

Read Luke 10:1-3

<u>*Key Verses*</u>*: "He told them, 'The harvest is plentiful, but the workers are few. Ask the Lord of the harvest, therefore, to send out workers into his harvest field. Go! I am sending you out like lambs among wolves.'" (Verses 2-3)*

"On your marks, set, go!" The starter's gun has fired and the race is on! Nobody has any doubt about the meaning of "go." You don't have the runners standing around asking questions like, "Well, *where* do we go?" or "Excuse me, but is this the 100-meters or 200-meters?" They know exactly what's expected of them and they respond accordingly.

That's because people who are told to "go" usually have a clear idea of what the speaker has in mind. The word often carries negative or harsh associations, as in "Ambrose, go to the principal's office right now." Or maybe brusque, as in one EMT to another: "Go get the defibrillator, now!" No time for "please" and "thank you."

Time for a brief grammar lesson. These examples we've seen of the word "go" are all in what's called the "imperative mood." In English the imperative is either a direct command or a strong request. So when we come to instances of "go" in the Bible we need to grasp the sense of importance the word typically conveys. That's why this is the only reflection in this book whose title has an exclamation mark. Why? To convey the sense of urgency or directness of the command.

The imperative sense of "go" comes up repeatedly throughout the Bible. We'll look at two examples from the Old Testament and then focus on several of Jesus' statements.

Let's begin with Moses. Having worn down God's patience with all his excuses, he hears this command: "The LORD said to him, 'Who gave human beings their mouths? Who makes them deaf or mute? Who gives them sight or makes them blind? Is it not I, the LORD? Now go; I will help you speak and will teach you what to say.'" (Ex. 4:11-12) This use of "go" puts an end to the back and forth they've been engaged in. Or at least it should. But then we read in the next sentence that Moses has the audacity to tell Yahweh, "Please send someone else." (Ex. 4:13) Well, at least he says "please…"

Then in another direct encounter between man and God, we have the awe-inspiring exchange between Isaiah and Yahweh, in which the prophet is aware of his deep unfitness in the presence of God's holiness. But after the angel cleans Isaiah's lips and fits him for service, God Himself tells Isaiah: "Go and tell this people…" (Is. 6:9)

"Go" appears often in Jesus' vocabulary. Here is a selection of Jesus' statements that reflect His authority, including over the disciples, those He has healed, or those trying to trap Him:

- To the demon-possessed man He healed: "Go home to your own people and tell them how much the Lord has done for you, and how he has had mercy on you." (Mk. 5:18-20)
- To the disciples, after His resurrection: "He said to them, 'Go into all the world and preach the gospel to all creation.'" (Mk. 16:15)
- To the disciples: "He told them, 'The harvest is plentiful, but the workers are few. Ask the Lord of the harvest, therefore, to send out workers into his harvest field. Go! I am sending you out like lambs among wolves.'" (Lk. 10:2-3)
- To the lawyer wanting to know who his neighbor was: "The expert in the law replied, 'The one who had mercy on him.' Jesus told him, 'Go and do likewise.'" (Lk. 10:37)
- To the woman caught in adultery: "'Then neither do I condemn you,' Jesus declared. 'Go now and leave your life of sin.'" (Jn. 8:11)
- To a man born blind: "'Go,' he told him, 'wash in the Pool of Siloam' (this word means 'Sent'). So the man went and washed and came home seeing." (Jn. 9:7)

~~~~~

In each of these six examples we see the authority that typifies Jesus' "go" statements. He didn't speak with a bossiness or domineering demeanor. He didn't need to, for He spoke and taught with a difference. As Mark tells us: "The people were amazed at his teaching, because he taught them as one who had authority, not as the teachers of the law." (Mk. 1:22)

Normally when imperative verbs are used, there's an assumption that the instruction is directed as someone right there, either you or me, or maybe both of us. Consequently, each of these persons whom Jesus was addressing had no doubt that they were the target of His instruction.

But there are times when "go" is not used as an instruction or request, as we see in this exchange between Jesus and the twelve disciples. Note Peter's answer: "From this time many of his disciples turned back and no longer followed him. 'You do not want to leave too, do you?' Jesus asked the Twelve. Simon Peter answered him, 'Lord, to whom shall we go? You have the words of eternal life. We have come to believe and to know that you are the Holy One of God.'" (Jn. 6:66-69)

When we therefore hear the Holy One of God telling us "Go!" we should be off and running. We should not emulate Moses' list of excuses or, worse still, after being given a clear "Go!" we remain in our starting blocks.

Hedged In

Read Job 3:23

<u>*Key Verse*</u>*: "Why should a man be born to wander blindly, hedged about by God on every side?" (Verse 23,* Revised English Bible)

It's one thing to be down on your luck or feeling totally directionless in life, like Job after the devastating series of misfortunes that God allowed to befall him. It's quite another to feel that it's God Who's behind it, that *God* is the one responsible for hedging you in.

As with the brutal honesty we encounter in the Psalms, so too does the book of Job pour out the despair of a man whose life has been shattered. He's stumbling around, unsighted spiritually, having stated earlier his regret that he was ever born. By anyone's standards, his life is truly a misery. Still, he acknowledges that God is there, perplexing though his Lord's conduct toward Job may be. He feels he has nowhere to turn; he's fenced in, like a bird in a cage, and it's God Who has set up this barrier.

His reaction is that of anger; the hedge is compounding his misery. But let's go back two chapters, where in their conversation about Job, God permits Satan to test this godly man. God says, "Have you considered my servant Job? There is no one on earth like him; he is blameless and upright, a man who fears God and shuns evil." (Job 1:8)

Satan's response is basically "Well, what do you expect, the way you look out for him." As he puts it, "Have you not put a hedge around him and his household and everything he has?" (Job 1:10) Satan resents this "hedge of protection."

Two chapters later, following all the misery that has resulted for Job with the loss of his family and physical possessions, it's Job's turn to recognize the hedge. But he sees it quite differently. He doesn't realize it's there for his spiritual protection, in effect keeping Satan from claiming the man himself. Now he is stumbling around, blind in his understanding of what God has permitted in his life, and because of his blindness is wandering at his peril. But for his safety, God is aware of Job's limited ability at this awful time in his life and hedged him in for his protection.

Job, poor man, thus carries a double burden on his faith journey with God. First, he is blinded to God's purposes for him. How awful it is to undergo the barrage of tragedies that he did, only to have them compounded by a total inability to see where his God is leading him, if anywhere. What is the point of all this, he's entitled to ask himself. Is this the life that God has for me?

The second burden is Job's sense that God Himself is actively working against him. *The Message* captures both these emphases well: "What's the point of life when it doesn't make sense, when God blocks all the roads to meaning?" (Job 3:23, *The Message*)

After hitting the deepest despair, he begins to get something of an answer from God. Beginning in chapter 38, God responds, essentially telling Job, "You have no idea what I, the God of all creation, am up to. You don't know why I allowed you to hit these roadblocks, why you ran out of gas, why you got stuck in the mud. Just know that I'm in charge."

Job's journey then turns positive, even though he cannot understand why God allowed him to be treated so miserably. St. Teresa of Ávila is credited with saying some version of this sentiment about God: "If this is how you treat your friends, it is no wonder you have so few!"[72] Even though Job didn't realize it, God was befriending him the entire time. For us, then, during those dark days on the journey it would be well to think of Job-like hedges, placed around us by the grace of God to prevent our situation from getting even worse.

---

[72] There is disagreement over the exact wording she is supposed to have said but this version will do for our purposes.

Leaping

Read 2 Samuel 22:1-51

<u>Key Verse:</u> *"...by my God have I leaped over a wall." (Verse 30,* King James Version)[73]

This verse struck Eugene Peterson so forcefully that it prompted him to write a book titled *Leap Over a Wall: Reflections on the Life of David*. In the introduction, he writes:

> *The image of David vaulting the wall catches and holds my attention. David running, coming to a stone wall, and without hesitation leaping the wall and continuing on his way — running toward Goliath, running from Saul, pursuing God, meeting Jonathan, rounding up stray sheep, whatever, but running. And leaping. Certainly not strolling or loitering.*[74]

Peterson captures well the energy and vitality of the young king-to-be. Maybe a good word to describe David is *brio*, which Merriam-Webster defines as "enthusiastic vigor, vivacity, verve."[75] All these terms describe a man whose aliveness is mirrored in his pursuit of God. Despite his stumbles (as noted in **Dancing** and **Detours**) he remains "a man after his [God's] own heart." (1 Sam. 13:14) The context is that Samuel is telling Saul he will forfeit his kingdom to David, because he is committed to Yahweh in a way that Saul is not.

We have a few other references to "leaping" in Scripture. One we have already discussed in **Dancing** (2 Sam. 6:16) Another is from the Song of Songs and is used poetically: "Listen! My beloved! Look! Here he comes, leaping across the mountains, bounding over the hills." (Song of Songs: 2:8)

Finally, we have two New Testament accounts. The first is when Elizabeth hears Mary's news that she is pregnant: "As soon as the sound of your greeting reached my ears, the baby in my womb leaped for joy." (Lk. 1:44) The second tells of the man lame from birth whom Peter heals, which the *King James Version* renders as: "And he leaping up stood, and walked, and entered with them into the temple, walking, and leaping, and

---

[73] This verse in 2 Samuel is part of a psalm by David, which is also recorded — in almost identical from — in Psalm 18.

[74] Eugene Peterson, *Leap Over a Wall: Reflections on the Life of David*, 11.

[75] https://www.merriam-webster.com/dictionary/brio. Accessed May 18, 2024.

praising God." (Acts 3:8) The *New International Version* has "jumped to his feet..."

What can we deduce from these biblical references to "leaping"? For one thing, there's the obvious point: these references are few and far between. We don't read much about biblical leaping. But a second thing to note is that in each instance we witness a sense of joy and high-spiritedness. With David writing that he leaps over a wall, there's a clear correlation with his military strength and triumph. There's a confidence and sense of gratitude to God that runs throughout the psalm. The reference to his leaping and dancing as he returns to Jerusalem with the ark (2 Sam. 6:16) flows from his sheer joy as he celebrates this momentous occasion.

Likewise, we see the joy of the bridegroom as he "leaps across mountains," the young lover seemingly walking on air. And the same response with the lame man who finds himself, for the first time in his life, able to do what the vast majority of us take for granted: he is, through God's grace and miraculous healing power, now able to walk.

The third point to make is that we can only rarely expect "leap-inducing" moments in our lives. It may be an occasion like the birth of a child, our wedding day, or the good news that there's no longer any trace of the cancer. Each of these moments is cause for celebration and over-the-top joy. Even if we don't physically leap around the delivery room or the hall that is holding the wedding reception, our hearts are leaping within us. These moments on the journey are the high points that may well make it into our obituaries one day. They are moments that propel us forward, with a blend of energy and verve. We feel we can jump any wall as we surge forward; we wouldn't even dream of strolling or loitering.

Limping

Read Genesis 32:22-32

Key Verse: *"The sun rose above him as he passed Peniel, and he was limping because of his hip." (Verse 31)*

When a friend from church was in the Navy decades ago, he was involved in a shipboard accident that led to his lower right leg being amputated. He now walks with a prosthesis and manages well. But there's no getting round the fact that his gait is impaired. He doesn't hobble, which one dictionary says is "to walk awkwardly and unsteadily by taking short unsteady steps."[76] But his limp is obvious. Nor can it be remedied, unlike someone who has a sprained ankle, for example, which will heal over time.

No, my friend's limp is now a part of who he is. One could say it's part of his identity, just as it was for Jacob. Following that mysterious night when he wrestled with God, who appears to have taken the form of an angel, his hip is injured — probably thrown out of joint and causing a permanent injury.

What are we to make of this strange episode? One lesson is that we shouldn't expect to wrestle with God and come away unchanged. Speaking in the context of God judging His people, the writer of Hebrews says, "It is a dreadful thing to fall into the hands of the living God." (Heb. 10:31) To wrestle with Him is surely equally frightening. Jacob got off lightly, with only an injured hip.

But another aspect of his identity was affected too. We read that "the man said, 'Your name will no longer be Jacob, but Israel, because you have struggled with God and with humans and have overcome.'" (Gen. 32:28) His new name means something like "he struggles with God," a name that carries over to his people and to the very state of Israel that was founded in 1948. So the man now identified by his limp is also known by a new name, which explains how he acquired the limp in the first place.

A limp, whether permanent or temporary, signifies an impairment or pain. One still makes progress on one's journey, walking "awkwardly and unsteadily." Walking is more difficult than it used to be but one persists. After all, the only alternative is to quit. Maybe one needs to rest more often. Or as one ages and one's body changes, the impairment becomes

---

[76] https://chambers.co.uk/search/?query=hobble&title=21st. Accessed May 14, 2024.

harder to bear.

Elbert Hubbard says that at the end of your journey, "God will not look you over for medals, degrees or diplomas, but for scars"[77]—for those who have suffered for the faith. And no doubt also those who, like Jacob, have limped to the finish line.

---

[77] Quoted in Gordon S. Jackson: *Quotes for the Journey, Wisdom for the Way*, 115.

Mobile Again

Read Mark 2:3-12

<u>*Key Verse*</u>: *"He got up, took his mat and walked out in full view of them all."* *(Verse 12)*

The entries in this book address mostly some voluntary posture; we've chosen to sit, stand, walk or run. But here we have a man who has not chosen his immobility, a condition which is somehow bound up with his sin. Jesus sees this link between his physical and spiritual need and shatters it with His command, "Get up, take your mat and go home." (Mt. 9:7) While the story goes on to show how Jesus has the power to forgive sin, our interest is in a man so incapacitated that his friends have to carry him on his mat to the crowded house where Jesus is. Thwarted by the crunch of people, they engage in the demolition project that allows them to lower their friend through the ceiling.

Being paralyzed, he cannot even get to Jesus under his own power. This man's helplessness may mirror our own at times. We may be desperately ill, perhaps even unconscious. Or we may be so traumatized by an accident or combat that we are suffering from what is severe PTSD. Mentally and emotionally, we are drained to the point of being unable to function. Or perhaps we are spiritually depleted, suffering from that condition known as the dark night of the soul.

It is as if you have fitted an immobilizer to your car, to deter potential thieves. If someone were to get your car started, it would cut out after perhaps a hundred yards or so, with the thief unable to restart it. You feel like that car; you've cut out and it seems nothing can get you restarted; regarding your spiritual standing, you seem to be beyond help. The prophet Isaiah touches on spiritual darkness, and offers the antidote, when he says, "Who among you fears the LORD and obeys the word of his servant? Let the one who walks in the dark, who has no light, trust in the name of the LORD and rely on their God." (Is. 50:10)

Charles Spurgeon says: "My case is urgent. I don't see how I am to be delivered; but this is no business of mine. He who makes the promise will find ways and means of keeping it. It is mine to obey his commands; it is not mine to direct his counsels. I am his servant... He will deliver."[78]

Yes, we may be totally immobilized, for whatever reason, but we can be assured that even in the darkest hour we can, and must, "trust in the

---

[78] Quoted in *Streams in the Desert*, 147.

name" of our LORD. We can rely on the One who in the long run will tell us to take up the mat that symbolizes our paralysis and go home.

Mountaintops

Read Matthew 17:1-8

Key Verse: *"After six days Jesus took with him Peter, James and John the brother of James, and led them up a high mountain by themselves." (Verse 1)*

~~~~~

"We cannot live forever in the moment on the mountain, but we cannot live at all without it."

— William Barclay[79]

"Mountaintop experiences" are a standard part of many Christians' vocabularies. They're a metaphor for those moments when we have an intimate encounter with God. Biblical examples include Moses on his several trips up Mount Sinai to meet with the living God and receiving the Ten Commandments. In the New Testament the preeminent mountaintop experience is Jesus' meeting with Moses and Elijah in a transfiguration witnessed by Peter, James and John.[80] Those experiences, treated in the reflection **Thin Places**, are rare. Many more of us will occasionally experience spiritual high points in our lives, where God seems especially close to us. They differ mostly in degree from those that occur in **Thin Places**. In the examples of Moses' and Jesus' experiences, it's noteworthy that they occurred on mountaintops. The focus in this reflection is on the setting of those experiences, whereas in **Thin Places** the emphasis is more on the transformation of Moses and Jesus.

One reason that mountaintop experiences are infrequent, although not as rare as what occurs in Thin Places, is that mountaintops are not hospitable places. As Craig Barnes points out,

> *It only takes a few minutes on the top of a high mountain for one to know just why God so frequently chose this setting. High peaks are barren, intimidating places. People don't belong up there. There is nothing to protect them — no trees, no shelter, just the wind and the uncomfortably thin air... To stand on the mountaintop is to place ourselves in the hands of forces and powers we cannot control or even resist. Centuries of religious experience have taught us that we are most capable of hearing God when we know how exposed we really are.*[81]

~~~~~

[79] William Barclay, *Daily Study Bible: The Gospel of Luke*, 126.
[80] Mt. 17:1-8. The transfiguration is also recorded in Mark and Luke.
[81] Craig Barnes: *Yearning*, 105.

Mountaintop experiences, both by design and by preference, are not the norm. God initiates them; we don't. Nowhere in Scripture do we find examples of people instigating such experiences. Oh, we may well initiate trips into **Deserts** or other places of seclusion to be with God, as Jesus Himself did. But those rare encounters with God on the peak are unexpected and unplanned. When they occur, we stay on the peak only as long as necessary, to receive instructions, inspiration, or whatever else God seeks to convey to us.

Those peak experiences can come unexpectedly, perhaps during the church choir's special music on Sunday, or a word in the sermon. When these "God moments" enter our lives, they may not have the earth-shaking quality of the transfiguration but will nevertheless profoundly touch us. Let us conclude with a word from Oswald Chambers: "We cannot stay on the mount of transfiguration, but we must obey the light we received there."[82]

Obedience is the key. For all the ecstatic experiences we may have in our faith, if they don't translate into practical ways of living out our faith, we might as well not have experienced them. The great nineteenth century theologian, Cardinal John Henry Newman, wrote, "I sought to hear the voice of God and climbed the topmost steeple, but God declared: 'Go down again—I dwell among the people.'"[83] Mountaintop or steeple-top experiences need to be followed by obedience to God's command to "go down again" and dwell among His people.

For a short while we will have been to the top of a mountain, where we received an infusion of the grace without which Barclay says "we cannot live at all." But it is grace that is to be shared, not hoarded, after we "go down again."

---

[82] Oswald Chambers: *My Utmost for His Highest*, March 22.
[83] https://www.goodreads.com/author/quotes/24706.John_Henry_Newman. Cited Oct. 5, 2024.

Night Driving

Read Exodus 13:20-22

<u>*Key Verse*</u>: *"By day the LORD went ahead of them in a pillar of cloud to guide them on their way and by night in a pillar of fire to give them light, so that they could travel by day or night." (Verse 21)*

Imagine you're driving on a country road on a dark night. Your car's headlights are illuminating what lies immediately ahead, giving you an accurate and trustworthy picture of reality. But what of the terrain lying 100 yards to the left or the right? You can have little idea of what lies outside your illuminated line of sight.[84] But you know you can rely on your lights to stay safely on the road immediately ahead of you.

It is the same with our spiritual journeys. We can be confident of the revelation God has made known to us—that is, the road immediately in front of us. In other words, we are given enough for our present needs.

Spiritually, Christians can thus be utterly confident in their belief that God's presence is with us in invisible and unknown ways. Moreover, that presence is by definition *good*. What we cannot see at present, as well as what lies ahead in our Christian journey, is unimaginably good, as Paul assures the Ephesians: "Now to him who is able to do immeasurably more than all we ask or imagine, according to his power that is at work within us...." (Eph. 3:20) Or, as Ben Patterson writes, "God is up to something so big, so unimaginably good that your mind cannot contain it... What we see God doing is never as good as what we don't see."[85]

---

[84] I am indebted to my Whitworth University colleague Professor James Edwards for this analogy.

[85] Quoted in Gordon S. Jackson: *Quotes for the Journey, Wisdom for the Way*, 64.

Pilgriming

Read Psalm 84:5
<u>*Key Verse*</u>*: "Blessed are those whose strength is in you, whose hearts are set on pilgrimage." (Verse 5)*

~~~~~

Pilgrimages: "Journeys to holy places undertaken from motives of devotion in order to obtain supernatural help or as acts of penance or thanksgiving."[86]

~~~~~

The concept of "pilgrim" or "pilgrimage" in Scripture is a paradox, as it appears only twice in the *New International Version*,[87] yet is a theme that runs throughout the Bible. Some form of "pilgrim" appears almost as infrequently (only five times) in the *King James Version*.[88] (Before we move on, be assured that the noun "pilgrim" can be made into a verb, "to pilgrim,"[89] a legitimate but rare usage.)

The entire biblical narrative is about pilgrimage. We Christians are all on a lifelong journey steeped in devotion to a God Who has saved us from our sin, and on Whom we rely for guidance, strength and protection—all in a way that is in a real sense supernatural. As the definition above indicates, pilgrimages can be literal, like a trip to Lourdes in the hope of healing. Or they can represent the lifelong journey of faith.

Although nowadays the word can loosely mean anyone who travels, the more precise and more traditional meaning is people who undertake pilgrimages for religious reasons. One such pilgrim in recent times is Shirley du Boulay, who went on a pilgrimage in England from Salisbury Cathedral to Canterbury. She described in her book, *The Road to Canterbury*, both what prompted her to make the pilgrimage with three friends, and the impact it had on her. Her account of the twelve days it took to cover the 130 miles between the two cathedrals is filled with reflections on her own journey, as well as the nature of pilgrimages in general. For example, she describes how in medieval times a pilgrim would do the following before setting out:

> *[He] would, before his departure, seek the permission of his wife, his parish priest and his feudal lord; he would make his will, set his*

---

[86] *The Concise Oxford Dictionary of the Christian Church*, 402.
[87] Gen. 47:9 and Ps. 84:5.
[88] Gen.47:9, Ex 6:4, Ps.119:54, Heb. 11:13 and 1 Pet. 2:11.
[89] https://en.wiktionary.org/wiki/pilgrim#Verb. Accessed May 27, 2024.

affairs in order and — most importantly, make amends to anyone he had wronged. He would probably have attended Mass, then, at either a public or private ceremony, he would receive a formal blessing ... in which his clothes, his wallet and mantle, his emblems, rucksack and staff, would also be blessed.[90]

In medieval times it was clearly a big deal to embark on a pilgrimage. Much of the earnestness with which pilgrims undertook this venture has continued. Think for example of the estimated 200,000 people who walk the famous Camino de Santiago trail, the "Way of St. James," in a given year. Not everyone does the full length of the nearly 500-mile trail, which begins in Saint-Jean-Pied-de-Port, on the French side of the Pyrenees and ends in the cathedral of Santiago de Compestela in the northern-Spanish city of Galicia. For these pilgrims, the primary goal is presumably spiritual enrichment.

Then there's the kind of journey we associate with people traveling to Lourdes, in the hope of some kind of healing. Also in southern France, in the foothills of the Pyrenees, this site draws millions of visitors a year. In 1858 the Virgin Mary is said to have appeared to a local woman, thus giving the town instant credibility as a potential site for a much-needed miracle of one's own.

~~~~~

So what are we to learn from these diverse pilgrims and their quests? The most important lesson is that a pilgrimage is a metaphor for our entire Christian journey. John Bunyan's famous allegory, *Pilgrim's Progress*, provides a picture of the Christian life as a journey that will culminate in heaven. That is the ultimate holy place toward which we are heading. Writers like Peter Kreeft have emphasized the notion that heaven is our ultimate home. He says, "Like the great mythic wanderers, like Ulysses and Aeneas, we have been trying to get home. Earth just doesn't smell like home... Heaven is."[91]

Bunyan's hymn, "To Be A Pilgrim," describes various circumstances that can deflect us from our course or hazards that we might encounter on the way. His own Christian journey included imprisonment on two occasions for his Puritan views, once for twelve years.

Dated though the language is, the hymn introduces us to the kind of barriers or pitfalls that may mark our pilgrimage and, more importantly, the protection with which God will surround us.

He who would valiant be
'gainst all disaster,

---

[90] Shirley du Boulay: *The Road to Canterbury*, 21.
[91] Peter Kreeft: *Heaven: The Heart's Deepest Longing*, 39.

let him in constancy
follow the Master.
There's no discouragement
shall make him once relent
his first avowed intent
to be a pilgrim.

Who so beset him round
with dismal stories,
do but themselves confound —
his strength the more is.
No foes shall stay his might,
though he with giants fight;
he will make good his right
to be a pilgrim.

Since, Lord, Thou dost defend
us with Thy Spirit,
we know we at the end
shall life inherit.
Then, fancies, flee away!
I'll fear not what men say,
I'll labor night and day
to be a pilgrim.[92]

~~~~~

What we could call a lifelong pilgrimage and a literal one have certain qualities in common. There is an overriding sense of purpose and a fixed focus on heading toward a destination. Both journeys are marked by an openness to learning more about God and oneself. Both types of pilgrimage face potential dangers and hostility along the way. (Du Boulay notes that in 1350 fully half of pilgrims to Rome were robbed or killed.[93]) Modern pilgrimages are far safer but nonetheless are hardly risk-free.

Then there's the need for "constancy" in our pilgrimage, as Bunyan puts it. It's not an everyday word; "faithfulness," "loyalty," or "steadiness" might be better alternatives for twenty-first century Christians. A related idea, again referring to Bunyan, is that having committed ourselves to either a short-term or a lifelong pilgrimage requires constant effort, the need "to labor day and night, to be a pilgrim."

~~~~~

Let's return to Shirley du Boulay and her pilgrimage, which began at

---

[92] https://hymnary.org/text/he_who_would_valiant_be. Accessed May 22, 2024.
[93] Shirley du Boulay: *The Road to Canterbury*, 15.

Salisbury Cathedral. She writes, "following the tradition of the medieval pilgrims, we went to St. John's, the oldest surviving parish church in Winchester." There, the vicar blessed the pilgrimage she and her friends were to pursue. He prayed for:

> … *a support in setting out, a solace on the way, a shadow in the heat, a cover from the rain and cold, a chariot in weariness, a protection in danger, a staff in slippery places, a harbor in shipwreck, that under your guidance they may happily reach the place whither they are going, and at length return to their homes in safety.*[94]

Du Boulay and her companions did in fact return home safely, when they had to adjust to their post-pilgrimage situation: "We were resuming our day-to-day lives, our journeys of perpetual pilgrimage."[95] That is perhaps the most important aspect of going on a pilgrimage: to better equip you for the life you will resume afterwards, a life that is now shaped by a richer understanding of God and yourself. A short-term pilgrimage is somewhat artificial, because by definition it isn't something one can do indefinitely. But its value includes providing spiritual food for the longer journey.

The actor and filmmaker Emilio Estevez says, "We don't think about pilgrimage in this country [the United States]. We don't think about meditation. The idea of taking a six-week walk is totally foreign to most Americans. But it's probably exactly what we need."[96] Shirley du Boulay would no doubt agree.

---

[94]Ibid, 20.

[95] Ibid, 232.

[96] https://www.brainyquote.com/topics/pilgrimage-quotes. Accessed May 27, 2024.

Placed[97]

Read Psalm 16:5-6

Key Verse: "The boundary lines have fallen for me in pleasant places; surely I have a delightful inheritance." (Verse 6)

When Fidel Castro was still prime minister of Cuba, a Presbyterian woman living under the tight restrictions of this Communist government undertook a speaking tour in the United States. In one church she emphasized how she believed that God had not placed her and other Christians in their country by mistake, and that He had a clear purpose for them being where they were at that difficult time.

As the saying goes, "Everybody's gotta be some place." Christians, though, accept that they are in places assigned by God, not by chance. The place where we spend all our time—or almost all of it—is the valley. We on rare occasions may ascend to a **Mountaintop** encounter with God. Or we may initiate a trip to the **Deserts** or find ourselves unwillingly thrust into one. But the norm is life in the valley.

Wherever you make home right now is not a coincidence. This is where God has placed you: to grow in grace, to minister, to be a witness to Him. It is here, and now, we are to be God's people. Jean-Pierre de Caussade says, "The whole essence of the spiritual life consists in recognizing the designs of God for us for *the present moment.*"[98] (Emphasis added.)

We may want to move to another valley, convinced that God has little or no use for us here. Maybe. Maybe you are hearing a call elsewhere. Or perhaps you're tired, bored or frightened and however you rationalize it, you want to turn your back on God's work in this place. Warren Wiersbe is helpful here: "If our service for the Lord doesn't make us grow, two things may be true: either we're in the wrong place, or we have the wrong attitude toward the right place."[99] Whether it's time to move to another valley, that's for you to figure out, with God's help.

As you explore your options, it might be fruitful to reflect on Benedictine monks, who upon entering a monastery take a vow of stability. This is a commitment to remain in the same monastery for the

---

[97] This section is adapted from Gordon S. Jackson: *Always Ready: A Christian Mandate*.
[98] https://www.firstthings.com/article/1998/02/the-school-of-sanctification. Accessed May 12, 2024.
[99] Warren Wiersbe: *On Being a Servant of God*, 58.

rest of their lives. (They take two others: a vow of faithfulness to the monastic way of life, and a vow of obedience. The requirements to live a life of poverty and chastity are assumed.) Not only can we learn from that degree of openness to accepting whatever their community will be like, we can learn too from the Apostle Paul, who told the Philippians, "For I, however I am placed, have learned to be independent of circumstances." (Phil. 4:11, *Twentieth Century Translation*)

Accept then, echoing the spirit of Paul, that your current valley is the place where you are to live out your faith, for now. As Oswald Chambers put it, "Never allow the thought, 'I am of no use where I am.' You certainly can be of no use where you are not."[100]

~~~~~

"God is here. Wherever we are, God is here. There is no place, there can be no place, where He is not."

— A. W. Tozer[101]

---

[100] Oswald Chamber, *My Utmost for His Highest*, Oct. 17.
[101] https://www.goodreads.com/quotes/7242047-wherever-we-are-god-is-here-there-is-no-place. Accessed May 12, 2024

Relocating

Read Ezekiel 3:22-23.

<u>*Key Verse*</u>*: "The hand of the LORD was on me there, and he said to me, 'Get up and go out to the plain, and there I will speak to you.'" (Verse 22)*

You've probably heard the story, from before we had GPS, about the city slicker who's driving in the countryside. He is lost and pulls over and asks a farmer how to get to his destination. The farmer responds, "You can't get there from here." It's an amusing but also a curiously provocative reply. Surely there has to be *some* way the city slicker can get where he's going. But what the farmer's really saying is, "This is not a good starting point for what you want to do."

That's exactly where Christians find themselves at times. Not that we are necessarily lost on our Christian journey, or that we have strayed from God. It's just that we're not yet in the right place to fulfill God's purposes for us. Ezekiel has that experience when God says to him in effect, "I'm glad you're paying attention; I have something more to tell you. But here's not the place to do that. Meet me on the plain."[102] Or, as *The Message* has it, "God grabbed me by the shoulder and said, 'Get up. Go out on the plain. I want to talk with you.'"

Why God doesn't deliver His message right then isn't clear. By obeying God, however, and going to the plain, Ezekiel has a profound experience of God and His holiness, as we read in verse 23.

Another example of someone being told to go elsewhere to hear God's instructions is the Apostle Paul. In recounting his dramatic conversion experience, he says that after being struck blind, he asked: "What shall I do, Lord?" The answer? "'Get up,' the Lord said, 'and go into Damascus. There you will be told all that you have been assigned to do.'" (Acts 22:10)

We should not expect experiences comparable to Ezekiel's and Paul's. And we should certainly not expect the mysterious experience of Philip upon baptizing the Ethiopian eunuch. Acts tells us, "When they came up out of the water, the Spirit of the Lord suddenly took Philip away, and the eunuch did not see him again, but went on his way rejoicing. Philip, however, appeared at Azotus..." (Acts 8:39-40) Philip is, quite literally, Spirited away to a new location. There, we are told, he "traveled about, preaching the gospel in all the towns until he reached Caesarea."

---

[102] Some translations say he is sent to the valley.

(Acts 8:40)

However, there may be times when God commands us, "Up; I need you elsewhere. Let's get moving. I'll tell you more when you get there." We have no right to demand His full set of instructions according to our schedule. As Matthew Henry put it, "Admirals, sometimes, when they are sent abroad, are not to open their commission till they have got so many leagues off at sea..."[103]

With God's leading, we *can* get there from here.

---

[103] Matthew Henry: *One-Volume Commentary on the Bible*, 1,145.

Rest and Rest Stops

Read Exodus 20:1-17

<u>Key Verses</u>: *"Remember the Sabbath day by keeping it holy. Six days you shall labor and do all your work, but the seventh day is a sabbath to the LORD your God. On it you shall not do any work, neither you, nor your son or daughter, nor your male or female servant, nor your animals, nor any foreigner residing in your towns. For in six days the LORD made the heavens and the earth, the sea, and all that is in them, but he rested on the seventh day. Therefore the LORD blessed the Sabbath day and made it holy."* (Verses 8-11)

The point of this book is to show how Christians move forward in their faith journeys in various ways. At various times we sit, or stand, or walk, or run. But there are also times to stop and "sharpen the saw," to use Steven Covey's example from his famous book, *The Seven Habits of Highly Effective People*. He describes someone who's cutting wood but using a saw whose blade has been dulled by use. The wood cutter is urged to take time out to sharpen the saw, but he insists he can't stop; he feels compelled to keep cutting despite doing so inefficiently and with far more effort than is needed. A few minutes taken to sharpen the saw would make life much easier.

How like us when we feel so pressured that we can't afford to stop sawing with our blunt saw. "Gotta keep going..."

~~~~~

A pastor supposedly had a sign on his desk that read, "Don't feel totally, personally, irrevocably responsible for everything; that's my job — God." Not a bad reminder about the limits of what God expects of you. This applies especially if you're in a setting where more and more people are turning to you for help, perhaps at work. Or perhaps you're under increasing pressure because of family obligations. Maybe a spouse is away on military service or for business, and you're alone taking care of your three preschool children. Or you're pastoring a congregation that seems to have infinite needs.

Isn't this what you are called to be doing? Isn't this unstinting service and making yourself available the very reason you seek to honor the Lord? Yes and no. Of course you want to follow Jesus' example of selfless ministry. Remember though that Jesus Himself set limits. Despite His boundless compassion He built into His routine ample time for prayer and solitude with His heavenly Father. Are you in danger of serving so much that you've developed a routine that is increasingly excluding the kind of prayer and solitude that Jesus modeled for us?

As you continue trying to define your calling, balance between your work and family life, or some next step in your ministry, keep asking what you think God is realistically expecting of you. As you work on your answer, bear in mind the warning of Thomas à Kempis, who wrote in *The Imitation of Christ* about certain over-eager saints of his day: "They presumed to do more than it was God's will for them to do, and so they soon lost the gift of grace."[104]

What is the antidote to the malady that à Kempis describes? The easy and obvious answer comes from the Ten Commandments, when Yahweh gave Moses a command to observe the sabbath—not a suggestion, not a thought to consider, but a *command*, for our wellbeing. At times, though, even that weekly respite may not be enough. A longer break from our ministry or calling may be required, as a writer in the devotional anthology, *Streams in the Desert*, points out: "Often the Lord calls us aside from our work for a season, and bids us be still and learn ere we go forth again and minister. There is no time lost in such waiting hours... So often God bids us tarry ere we go, and fully recover ourselves for the next stage of the journey and work."[105] The form this season of life takes can vary. It may be a time of unemployment or illness, neither of which we've signed up for. It may bear some resemblance to the sabbatical leave that academic institutions give faculty members, in that it's a temporary freedom from responsibilities to pursue one's own agenda for a while.

Whether it is observing a weekly sabbath or experiencing a months-long sabbatical, we do well to recall the words of Abraham Joshua Heschel, the rabbi and philosopher who says, "The sabbath is an oasis in time."[106] And possibly also a place that offers saw sharpening services.

---

[104] Thomas à Kempis: *The Imitation of Christ*, translation by Betty I, Knott, 122.
[105] *Streams in the Desert*, 161.
[106] Quoted in Gordon S. Jackson, *Quotes for the Journey, Wisdom for the Way*, 144.

"Returning Forward"

Read Luke 24:13-35

Key Verses: *"When he was at the table with them, he took bread, gave thanks, broke it and began to give it to them. Then their eyes were opened and they recognized him, and he disappeared from their sight. They asked each other, 'Were not our hearts burning within us while he talked with us on the road and opened the Scriptures to us?' They got up and returned at once to Jerusalem." (Verses 30-33)*

Someone once warned about returning to a favorite travel destination and expecting it to duplicate our previous experience: "Don't go back! It isn't there anymore. Exception: Switzerland."[107] Whether or not you agree with this assessment, it provides a helpful springboard for us to think about the well-known mysterious encounter the two disheartened disciples experienced en route to Emmaus. With the benefit of hindsight, we may chuckle over how they unwittingly engage in conversation with the risen Jesus. Then we encounter the equally mysterious "opening of their eyes" as they realize over their meal together who He is.

That's typically where our interaction with the story ends. But wait, as they say, there's more: What about their *return* trip? What can we learn from that?

Note how they realize the magnitude of their encounter and its demands for action. The one Who they thought was dead is alive, news of such importance that they do an immediate about turn. They had already walked the seven-mile trip from Jerusalem (see verse 13). Now, despite the onset of night and the danger that would attend travel in the dark, they unhesitatingly set out to return to Jerusalem.

Why? Because of their *response* to Jesus. Their encounter has transformed them, in at least six ways.

1. Their faith is revitalized, in a way they could never have imagined. Seeing the risen Jesus for themselves has boosted their faith in a way that the earlier and indirect reports of the resurrection could not.

2. Their faith empowers them. Previously they were dispirited. Now they are infused with the courage that drives them to undertake an arduous and dangerous journey in the dark, to confirm to the disciples in Jerusalem that those earlier rumors about Jesus are true.

---

[107] Quoted in Gordon S. Jackson, *The Weather is Here, Wish You Were Beautiful: Quotations for the Thoughtful Traveler*, 98.

3. Their status has changed. They are now eyewitnesses to the resurrection. Like a growing number of disciples, they have the authority or "street cred" to testify about what they have seen.

4. They now have a message to share, initially with the disciples but then more broadly as they testify to the resurrection.

5. They are driven to immediate action. What a contrast between their despondency when Jesus first comes alongside them, and the zeal with which they decide to make the return trip. They don't spend the rest of the evening merely pondering this wondrous experience, they act.

6. They reaffirm that they are part of "a fellowship of faith," as shown by their immediate return to the other disciples in Jerusalem, to share with them the astonishing news of their encounter with Jesus.

~~~~~

In the **Introduction** we cited Paul Tournier's comment that "The Holy Spirit is always calling us forward, not back."[108] The Emmaus story presents us with the Spirit calling these two disciples *forward* by taking them *back*. What are we to make of what sounds like a paradox? And how can we apply it to our lives?

One immediate benefit of "looking back" in our faith ties in with the concept of remembering. Repeatedly, the children of Israel are told to remember who they are, Who has called them, and what Yahweh has done for them in their covenant relationship. To cite but one of dozens of verses that underscore the importance of remembering, Yahweh says in Deuteronomy 5: "Remember that you were slaves in Egypt and that the LORD your God brought you out of there with a mighty hand and an outstretched arm." (Dt. 5:15)

A pastor once said that in times of crisis, when you don't know where else to turn, look back to the basics of your faith and seek assurance from what you know to be true. Just as the children of Israel were told repeatedly to remember what God had done for them, so too should we. That "rear-view mirror of faith" is there for a reason.

The Emmaus episode tells us that even if Switzerland never changes, two things that pertain to their situation are dramatically different. The disciples gathered in Jerusalem are now increasingly emboldened as more of them learn of Jesus' resurrection and are open to hearing the confirmation that these two disciples will bring from Emmaus. These two late-night travelers were changed into dramatically different people.

To Emmaus	From Emmaus
Jesus is with them	Jesus is not physically with them
They are Downcast	They are Overjoyed

---

[108] Paul Tournier: *The Adventure of Living*, 40.

It's a Time of Learning	It's a Time of Sharing
It's a Time of Spiritual Blindness	It's a New Chapter of Spiritual Awareness
"We had been hoping...."/If only	"He is the Risen Messiah!"
They are the hosts/the initiators	Now Jesus is the initiator

~~~~~

It is a good thing, then, to return to the roots of our faith, to reassert or remember our own covenantal relationship with God. The Bible provides repeated instructions to do exactly that, in a one-word instruction: *Remember*. The word appears 231 times in the *New International Version*, thus underscoring the importance of recognizing what we've learned on the journey so far, and to assure ourselves of the goodness of God that we've encountered over and over.

Recalling what we have learned is only part one, however; the clear assumption is that we'll act in response to what we've remembered. Our driving forward is to be shaped by what we remember.

But there is a potential danger of obsessing over one spiritual "high moment." Honor Gilbert, writing about the value of keeping a spiritual journal, described a man who went overboard and so fixated on one entry that he kept trying to re-live what for him was a spiritually profound moment. He wrote down a vivid account of his experience and frequently re-read it and fixated on it. Then, Gilbert writes, "One day he rushed down to his wife in great distress, 'The mice have eaten my blessed experience,' he cried."[109]

This poor man had three problems. First, he kept looking backward in his faith, not forward. He was uninterested in or open to the blessings that await, as that beloved passage in Lamentations notes, "Because of the Lord's great love we are not consumed, for his compassions never fail. They are new every morning; great is your faithfulness." (Lam. 3:22-23)

Yet we shouldn't be living out our faith journey with our eye constantly on the rear-view mirror, as if we'd almost prefer that God would return us to an earlier time. Yes, learning from and building upon our experiences of God is crucial as we move toward Christian maturity. But this poor fellow went beyond looking in the mirror; he had turned his car around to see where he'd come from.

Second, his was a self-absorbed faith, focusing on *his* experience, and what God had done for *him*. He was living out a Christian experience so narrowly defined that he precluded whatever else God had in store for him. He had done exactly what Oswald Chambers warned against: "not

---

[109] Edward England, *Keeping a Spiritual Journal*, 150.

to make a fetish of your rare moments."[110]

Unlike this man, we ought always to be focused on the road ahead, on what lies ahead in our earthly journey. Nevertheless, any good driver would also keep an eye on the rear-view mirror. As we glance at the mirror repeatedly, we need to ask, "Is anything happening behind us that we need to be aware of as we move forward?" But staring fixedly at the mirror is asking for trouble.

The man's third problem was getting rid of the mice.

---

[110] Oswald Chambers, *My Utmost for His Highest*, April 25.

The Road Ahead

Read Matthew 28:5-7

Key Verse: "*He has risen from the dead and is going ahead of you into Galilee. There you will see him.*" *(Verse 7)*

When the US President is about to travel an advance team goes ahead to ensure all kinds of logistical and security measures are in place. This entails everything from setting up metal detectors for those who will meet the President or be in the same setting, to ensuring an adequate supply of the President's blood type is on hand in case the President is injured or falls ill and needs surgery. The agents work with local and state law enforcement on security arrangements, as well as with the US military's bomb disposal units. In short, an extensive amount of preparation goes into even a brief stop, such as on an election campaign visit.

So what does that have to do with our Christian journey? We turn to Eugene Peterson for some insight. Reflecting on his duties as a pastor, he wrote that, "In every visit, every meeting I attend, every appointment I keep, I have been anticipated. The risen Christ got there ahead of me." He imagined how, for example, "'...he is going before you to 1,020 Emmorton Road; there you will see him, as he told you.' Later in the day it will be, 'He is risen, ... he is going before you to St. Joseph's Hospital; there you will see him, as he told you.'"[111]

Think of what you have lined up today: a meeting with the marketing committee, a doctor's appointment about that chronic back ache, a parent-teacher conference late this afternoon. Whatever it is, imagine Christ having gone before you. Realize too that He has been at work, preparing the ground for your arrival.

This was a theme in the Old Testament too. For example, we have Yahweh's assurance that He will prepare the way for them and clear the way for them. "The LORD your God, who is going before you, will fight for you, as he did in Egypt..." (Dt. 1:30)

This assurance that God goes ahead of us is especially comforting when we face major decisions and seek His guidance. It may be that we cannot easily decide between two or more courses of action. Or we may feel stymied and don't even know what our options are. F. B. Meyers speaks to this situation: "When you are doubtful as to your course, submit your judgment absolutely to the Spirit of God, and ask Him to shut against

---

[111] Eugene Peterson: *Living the Message*, Sept. 18.

you every door but the right one... As you go down the long corridor, you will find that He has preceded you, and locked many doors which you would fain [rather] have entered; but be sure that beyond these there is one which He has left unlocked."[112]

As Peterson says, "We are always coming in on something that is already going on... Always we are dealing with what the risen Christ has already set in motion." And encountering the doors He has gone ahead and unlocked for us.

---

[112] Quoted in *Streams in the Desert*, July 31.

Rudderless[113]

Read Genesis 6:9-8:22

Key Verses: "*For forty days the flood kept coming on the earth, and as the waters increased they lifted the ark high above the earth. The waters rose and increased greatly on the earth, and the ark floated on the surface of the water. They rose greatly on the earth, and all the high mountains under the entire heavens were covered." (Verses 7:17-19)*

~~~~~

Shirley Toulson, in her book *The Celtic Year,* says: "*They [Celtic pilgrims] were emulating Abraham, who left his settled homeland at the command of Yahweh, and like him they made no plans but trusted that God would direct their footsteps. We are told that they even went to sea rudderless, letting the currents, the tides, and the winds take them to a destination known only to God."[114]*

~~~~~

Nimitz-class aircraft carriers in the US Navy have two massive rudders, which are twenty-nine feet high and twenty-two feet long. Each weighs 110,000 pounds.[115] Each is presumably carefully designed to be commensurate with the needs of the massive vessels they guide. Just how crucial is a ship's control of steering was shown in March 2024. This is being written weeks after the Dali cargo ship crashed into a support of the Francis Key bridge in Baltimore, MD, in the middle of the night. Six construction workers on night shift tumbled from the bridge to their deaths. At this point it appears the ship had an electrical system failure, which among other things didn't allow it to steer properly. But whatever the reason, it was a dramatic and tragic demonstration of what can go wrong when a vessel can no longer steer. In addition to the lives lost, the cost to replace the bridge will run to more than $1 billion.

One of the Bible's few references to rudders, and their importance, comes in James' epistle. The context is the power of the human tongue, a small part of us that can cause immense damage if not controlled. James

---

[113] This reflection is adapted from Gordon S. Jackson, *Your Photo on God's Fridge Door.*

[114] Quoted in Shirley du Boulay: *The Road to Canterbury,* 148.

[115] https://en.wikipedia.org/wiki/Nimitz-class_aircraft_carrier#:~:text=The%20turbines%20power%20the%20four,pounds%20(50%20metric%20tons). Accessed May 18, 2024.

adds, "[T]ake ships as an example. Although they are so large and are driven by strong winds, they are steered by a very small rudder wherever the pilot wants to go." (Jas. 3:4) William Barclay quotes Aristotle on this concept, saying: "A rudder is small and it is attached to the very end of the ship, but it has such power that by this little rudder, and by the power of one man — and that a power gently exerted — the great bulk of ships can be moved."[116] It's impossible to imagine the captain of even the smallest vessel, let alone an aircraft carrier, setting out on a journey knowing its rudder was defective.

By contrast, compare the Celts' commitment to "rudderless-ness" that Shirley Toulson mentioned to Noah's adventure in the ark. Like the Celts who chose to go to sea without a rudder, he too drifted rudderless, afloat for nearly a year before the ark ended its voyage on Mount Ararat.

We humans, however, are typically not excited about the idea of being rudderless. Probably Noah wasn't either. Living as we do in an era of GPS directions, we depend on our smartphones to tell us to turn left in 100 yards or that "Your destination is on your right." The idea of beginning a journey without our phone would make many of us uncomfortable; doing so without even having a **Destination** in mind is unthinkable.

Curiously, we are told considerable detail about Noah's preparation in building the ark. We learn its dimensions, how many decks it was to have (three) and the type of wood he was to use — cypress, according to the *New International Version*. Other translations have cedar, gopher or pine; it's okay, Noah would have known. Yet Genesis tells us virtually nothing about the extended time afloat. That's most likely because nothing much happened day after day after bleak and boring day, until after nearly a year Noah sends out a raven and then a dove to scout out the land, or more precisely to discover if there *is* any land.

What a boring, uneventful journey that must have been. Yet the tedium was the price to pay for saving a godly man and his family, just as William Warburton says is the value of the church: "The church, like the Ark of Noah, is worth saving, not for the sake of the unclean beasts and vermin that almost filled it, and probably made most noise and clamor in it, but for the little corner of rationality that was as much distressed by the stink within as the tempest without."[117]

So there are times when God may ask us to do something similar: stick with Him on a boring, noisy, smelly journey, for who knows how long, with no clear destination. In fact, that could be *exactly* what He calls us to. We can have no assurance that we will reach the destination we

---

[116] William Barclay: *The Daily Study Bible: The Letters of James and Peter*, 84.
[117] Quoted in Gordon S. Jackson: *Quotes for the Journey, Wisdom for the Way*, 38.

think we're sailing toward. The God-ordained currents, tides and winds in our lives may override whatever control we think we have of our rudder. Like Jonah, we may think we're heading in one direction (disregard for the moment that he was acting out of disobedience), yet God's true destination for him was in the opposite direction: Nineveh. Even when we've set our sails to honor what we believe God's will to be, we may be in for surprises.

"Are you willing to leave your phone, GPS and compass behind?" God asks. "And don't worry about the lack of a rudder. I know where we're going. Trust me." We echo the words of Polish poet Wisława Szymborska, winner of the Nobel Prize for literature, who wrote, "An endless rain is just beginning. Into the Ark, for where else can you go."[118] Where indeed.

~~~~~

I know I cannot drift
Beyond his love and care.

— *John Greenleaf Whittier*

---

[118] chrome-extension://efaidnbmnnnibpcajpcglclefindmkaj/ https://www.mcadmanila.org.ph/wp-content/uploads/2016/10/SAFE-PLACE-Study-Guide.pdf. Accessed May 22, 2024.

Shelter and Safety En Route

Read Psalm 91
<u>Key Verse</u>: *"If you say, 'The* LORD *is my refuge,' and you make the Most High your dwelling, no harm will overtake you, no disaster will come near your tent." (Verse 9)*

~~~~~

First, there is the recognition that disaster may touch us at any moment. Yet whatever our circumstances, we are assured that, in Christ, we need not be discouraged. By trusting fully in God and clinging to the peace He offers, we can have a disposition that will protect us from despair. In **Baby Steps** we cited Stephen Rankin's definition of spiritual maturity as having a certain set of dispositions, those "tendencies to act in certain ways under certain circumstances."[119] With the Holy Spirit's help, he says, we can act in Christ-like ways in the face of adversity.

Then, as we saw in **Pilgriming**, John Bunyan talks about fighting against giants. These threats also count for nothing; the Christian's God-given strength will prevail against even life's severest challenges. Bunyan explicitly says that God will defend us with His Spirit. Written in 1684, the hymn quoted previously has encouraged Christians for more than three centuries, reminding them both that they will encounter difficulties in their pilgrimage *and* that God will help them overcome whatever they face.

Let's dig a little deeper. We'll look at five themes concerning the protection that God affords His people. The first is the wide range of biblical images that describe this protection. The Bible offers us an abundance of images describing God's concern and protection for us as we journey in His company. The Psalms in particular sing the praises of a God who is our shield. "[Y]ou, LORD, are a shield around me..." (Ps. 3:3). Again in Psalm 18:2, additional images remind us of God's varied ways of protecting us: "The LORD is my rock, my fortress and my deliverer; my God is my rock, in whom I take refuge, my shield and the horn of my salvation, my stronghold."

In this one verse alone, we have rock (twice), fortress, deliverer, shield, horn of salvation, and stronghold. All of these terms are defensive and play a protective role. The "horn of salvation," commentators agree,

---

[119] Stephen Rankin: *Aiming at Maturity*, 16.

refers to the power of the king.[120]

"Shield" deserves special attention, occurring as it does twenty-two times in the *New International Version* of the Psalms, virtually all of them referring to God's protection rather than actual physical shields. A shield is a device to protect you from an attacker. To state the obvious, a shield provided to you is of no use until you strap it to your arm to fend off an attacker. God's provision of a shield is meaningless until we play our part by strapping it on and using it to block the enemy's weapon. What might such a "spiritual shield" look like in our day? At the very least, it is a combination of prayer, a grasp of Scripture that assures us of God's care and protection, and an unswerving faith that God "shields all who take refuge in him."[121]

A second theme offers an uncomfortable contrast. There's the inexplicable mystery, it seems, that sometimes God's protection fails. After all, Christians, no less than anyone else, are not spared death in traffic accidents, tornadoes or military combat. Why is the pilgrimage of this young Christian cut tragically short by illness? Or why is that father of three young children killed in a drive-by shooting? Where was God's protection when it was most needed? Had God run out of shields because of supply chain issues? Like the psalmist, we can dare to ask these questions. But like Job, we need to be satisfied with God's response, that Job has no idea what God is doing.[122] In matters like these, we read in *The Interpreter's Bible*, "It is always exceedingly difficult to get a direct answer from God."[123] We are to accept in faith that God is in charge and that despite appearances His love is undiluted and always present, whether we sense His protection or not.

A third theme concerns peace of mind. Thus far our emphasis has been on physical safety while on our spiritual journey. We pray for "traveling mercies" when going on a physical trip, to protect us from accidents, illness, or whatever else could threaten our personal wellbeing. But there's also the need to be free from worry. Richard Lovelace says, "Anxiety is often a red light on the mind's dashboard that tells us we are not expressing our needs to God and trusting in his providence."[124] The antidote to worry and anxiety comes in Paul's words to the Philippians, assuring them that "the peace of God, which transcends all understanding, will guard your hearts and your minds in Christ Jesus."

---

[120] We encounter the term again in Luke's gospel, when Zechariah praises God for the arrival of his son, who was to become John the Baptist: "He has raised up a horn of salvation for us in the house of his servant David. (Lk. 1:69)

[121] Ps. 18:30.

[122] See **Hedged In**.

[123] *The Interpreter's Bible*, vol. 3, 1,170.

[124] Quoted in Gordon S. Jackson: *Quotes for the Journey, Wisdom for the Way*, 16.

(Phil. 4:7)

Fourth, we turn to the part that guardian angels play in God's care and protection of His people.[125] Let us look at Psalm 91, another chapter steeped in language about God's protection, but with the added mention of angelic help.

> *If you say, "The LORD is my refuge," and you make the Most High your dwelling, no harm will overtake you, no disaster will come near your tent. For he will command his angels concerning you to guard you in all your ways; they will lift you up in their hands, so that you will not strike your foot against a stone. You will tread on the lion and the cobra; you will trample the great lion and the serpent. (Ps. 91:9-13)*

There we have it: The promise of angels who will "guard you in all your ways." At the risk of overgeneralizing, Protestants downplay the role or even the presence of angels in our daily lives. Oh, they may show up like a FedEx delivery person at some point with a special message. But in general, they don't feature prominently in Protestant theology, assumptions or expectations. Catholics, by contrast, tend to accord angels a far more significant role. Catholic philosopher and theologian Peter Kreeft, for example, takes it as a given that we each have one or more guardian angels assigned to us, for our protection. "There are," he says, "twice as many persons we can see in every place, every kitchen or classroom, every hospital or nursery. Only half are *human* persons. There is an angel standing next to each bag lady. Think of that next time you pass one by."[126]

Regardless of our theology of guardian angels, of this we can be sure: we serve a God who is all-knowing (about us, our circumstances, our possible dangers), omnipotent (no hazard we may face can trump God's power), and infinitely loving (nothing can happen to us to take us outside God's love). Not a bad combination, that. We're assured of God's protection whether we believe in guardian angels or not.

The fifth theme may not be obvious as one of God's vehicles for protecting us but is crucially important nonetheless: our own resources. Our common sense, good judgment and instincts warn us to avoid potential hazards. We have been gifted with antennae that help us detect danger. If we're driving and see unexpected congestion ahead, we slow down. Common sense tells us not to walk in the worst part of town at three in the morning. We wash our hands after using the bathroom to

---

[125] This section on guardian angels is adapted from Gordon S. Jackson: *Ninety Days of Difference*.

[126] Peter Kreeft: *Angels and Demons*, 93.

ward off germs. None of these actions seem like a divinely inspired move. Yet each could be a lifesaver. No trumpets sound, no angels appear in time to save us. Our God-given sense does the job and that is enough.

~~~~~

In one way or another, we are blessed with an arsenal of protections on our pilgrimage. Like John Newton, we can look back on examples of those protections in our lives. And, as important, we can look to God's grace to "lead us home."

> *Through many dangers, toils and snares*
> *I have already come:*
> *'tis grace has brought me safe thus far,*
> *and grace will lead me home.*[127]

---

[127] https://hymnary.org/text/amazing_grace_how_sweet_the_sound. Accessed May 22, 2024.

Soaring

Read Isaiah 40

Key Verses: *"Even youths grow tired and weary, and young men stumble and fall; but those who hope in the* LORD *will renew their strength. They will soar on wings like eagles; they will run and not grow weary, they will walk and not be faint." (Verses 30-31)*

Eagles soar. We don't. Well, not literally. But first let's look at why the few Bible references to "soaring" are usually associated with eagles.[128]

Eagles have long drawn an understandable admiration and even reverence from us humans. They are majestic birds, gifted with great power, speed and strength. They can fly as high as 10,000 feet and are equipped with eyesight that dwarfs our own: they can see potential prey like a rabbit from up to two miles away.

It's no surprise then that from ancient times people have paid special attention to these birds. Sometimes we incorporate them into our symbols, as the United States has done with the bald eagle. We admire eagles for their freedom and dominance of their realm; they are to the world of birds what the lion is to the African savannah. Their ability to soar to great heights seems to bridge the gap between us earth-bound creatures and the heavens. It is no wonder that their feathers are coveted and incorporated into Native American culture in the US.

In short, eagles have many qualities that Christians can admire and seek to emulate. One of these is perspective. Gladys Aylward, a British missionary to China, says, "The eagle that soars in the upper air does not worry itself as to how it is to cross rivers."[129] Christians are empowered people, filled as we are with the Holy Spirit and equipped to do God's work, wherever we are **Placed**. At times we may reach spiritual heights, as we note in **Mountaintops** and **Thin Places**. But we are always "Spirit-powered," capable of "flying high" spiritually each day. If we were an eagle flying two miles above the earth, we'd not be fretting over how to cross a river. Likewise, we Christians at times need to remind ourselves of our identity as God's children, and Whom we serve. As Christ's

---

[128] The *New International Version* refers to eagles soaring, in addition to Is. 40:31, in 2 Sam. 22:11 (and Ps. 18:10, which mirrors 2 Sam. 22 almost exactly); Job. 39:27; and Ob. 1:4.

[129] https://www.azquotes.com/picturequote/16822. Accessed May 20, 2024.

ambassadors,[130] we are accorded the powers of the One we represent. It behooves us, then, to be living out our faith in a way that demonstrates an eagle-like confidence.

John Harris says, "He [God] looks into an immense future and sees what we cannot. God acknowledges our questions but invites us to trust him so that we can soar beyond all fear and doubt into his eternity."[131] As for needing to cross those rivers two miles below, we barely notice them.

---

[130] 2 Cor. 5:20.
[131] Scripture Union *Daily Bread* Bible reading notes, no date.

Solo Travel

Read Hebrews 10:24-25

Key Verses: "[L]et us consider how we may spur one another on toward love and good deeds, not giving up meeting together, as some are in the habit of doing, but encouraging one another (Verses 24-25)

Short Version: For Christians, solo travel is a bad, bad idea.

Longer Version: Even the best tennis players in the world have coaches. They know they need expert help to identify weaknesses in their game. Like the rest of us, these top performers can be blind to their flaws and need an objective outsider to point them out and suggest strategies for overcoming them. Christians too need each other, whether it's a friend with whom you get together for coffee once a month or a community of faith like your local church or a Bible study group. Regardless of the form it takes, each of us needs external support mechanisms to nurture and sustain our faith.

In short, Christians ought not to be solo travelers or spiritual Lone Rangers in their faith. It's noteworthy, for example, that when Jesus sent out seventy-two disciples on an evangelistic mission to share the good news of God's Kingdom, He made them go in pairs. (Lk. 10:1) Similarly, He said when two or three are gathered together, He would be there with them. (Mt. 18:20) Of course, we know that Jesus is with us individually as well. And on rare occasions we may find ourselves in settings where we have no other Christian company. For the most part, though, we can count on the presence of at least some Christian companionship on our faith journey.

Such companionship is vital for a flourishing Christian walk. We need encouragement from those who share our faith. At times we may need correction, or at least some kind of accountability. Or we may need help of some kind, or be in a position to give help, in thinking through some perplexing aspect of our faith. We also benefit from the richness of our Christian community, as well as serving as contributors to it. (Think for example of the important role the coffee hour after worship plays out in your church.)

It's no coincidence that Paul used the image of the church as a body, in which all of us are needed and interrelated. (1 Cor. 12:12-27) Indeed, we could say that our identity as an eye or an ear, or the head or the feet, is dependent on being connected with the body. An eye functioning as part of a body is a marvel of biology; apart from the body, perhaps having been

121

surgically removed, it is merely tissue to be disposed of in a hospital incinerator. Whatever our role in God's church, it is meaningful only to the extent that it *is* part of that body.

Some Christians for whatever reason elect not to commit to any one church. Or they may conclude after short dalliances with a succession of churches that none of them adequately meets their needs or their theology isn't quite right. Or the people are hypocritical. Whatever the reason, these spiritual Lone Rangers conclude that they're better off on their own. Apparently, they have never heard the adage that if you find the perfect church, you shouldn't join it because you'll ruin it. It's precisely because of their arrogance or self-righteousness that they need Christian fellowship as much as anyone.

With so many churches now live-streaming their services, it's even easier for this type of Christian to stay at home and, assuming they've found a church they otherwise like, choose to "attend" remotely. This way they avoid interacting with all those annoying folks during coffee hour. The fact is, however, that Christians need each other. The verse from Hebrews cited above makes clear that there's a danger associated with not meeting together. Not everyone is physically able to do so; poor health or frailty may make church attendance impossible. But a Christian who can attend church and elects not to is at risk of spiritual malnutrition. At the same time, Christians who think they can go solo on the journey God has set before them display a distinctive and especially ugly kind of spiritual hubris.

Which brings us back to the...

Short Version: For Christians, solo travel is a bad, bad idea.

By Stages

Read Genesis 13:1-4

Key Verse: "*From the Negeb he journeyed by stages towards Bethel...*" (*Verse 3*, Revised English Bible)

Abraham's life was extraordinary in that God called him out of a pagan environment to follow Him to an unknown Promised Land and to be a father of multitudes. As the father figure of the three great monotheistic faiths, Christianity, Judaism and Islam, he played a unique role in history.

Yet in one respect he was like the rest of us, living his life one step at a time. Also like us, he didn't have perfect clarity on his destination. Like us in yet another way, even this great man of God made his mistakes. (Lying to Pharaoh that Sarah was his sister was not the smartest of moves; doing it again with Abimelech[132] was even dumber.) Yet if there's one overriding legacy we can take from Abraham's life, it was that of a deep faith, a faith that led him by stages as he sought to respond to God's revelation, one God-directed step at a time.

Centuries later, we learn how Abraham's descendants are about to enter the Promised Land. Yahweh firmly instructs them to have nothing to do with the pagan nations they will encounter, who will constitute a formidable opposition as the Israelites try to take possession of the land. Yet He assures them that they will succeed. Then comes a curious verse, telling them neither to expect nor to pursue a blitzkrieg style takeover, in which they swiftly and decisively obliterate the enemy: "The LORD your God will drive out those nations before you, little by little. You will not be allowed to eliminate them all at once, or the wild animals will multiply around you." (Dt. 7:22)

First, notice that despite the opposition they will face, it is Yahweh Himself Who will secure the victory for them. It will not be their own merits or military prowess that does so. Second, He tells the Israelites that victory will be accomplished "little by little." Matthew Henry says of this verse that "God will do his own work in his own method and time, and we may be sure that they are always the best."[133] In this case God explains the reason (or at least, *a* reason) for this gradual approach. Depopulating

---

[132] Genesis 12:10 through 13:1, in the encounter with Pharaoh, and Genesis 20, in the encounter with Abimelech.
[133] Matthew Henry: *One-Volume Commentary on the Bible*, 183.

the land of the pagan peoples too quickly will open the door for wild animals to thrive, thus presenting a needless additional challenge to the Israelites as they settle the land.[134]

A gradual, step-by-step approach was called for, something that may go against the grain for us, as we live in a culture that demands things *now*, a culture epitomized by Amazon Prime's next day delivery. Or that our checked bags will arrive at carousel three within twenty minutes, guaranteed.

Then, in case we need it, there's the counsel of the French Jesuit, Teilhard de Chardin, who says, "Trust in the slow work of God."[135]

---

[134] Later, as we know, the Israelites failed to fully remove the peoples who inhabited the land, which resulted in recurring serious problems as they sought compromises with their pagan neighbors.

[135] Quoted in Greg Boyle: *Tattoos on the Heart*, 113.

Being Still

Read Psalm 46
<u>*Key Verse*</u>: *"Be still and know that I am God." (Verse 10)*

Being still is different from resting, waiting or merely vegging. Being still is purposeful. It is a deliberate act of concentrating on shutting out extraneous thoughts and claims on one's attention. You're not checking your emails, getting dinner ready, or using TurboTax to complete this year's taxes. You can't be still and multitask. The reason Christians sometimes need to be still comes in the rest of the verse, where God says: "I will be exalted among the nations, I will be exalted in the earth." We are given the reason for this command to be still. It is to know that the speaker is God Himself, the one Who will be exalted.

We can't do justice to focusing intensely on God if we're getting up or walking or running. Stillness must at times be built into our journey. The *New International Version* study notes for this verse say that the Hebrew for the phrase "be still" "probably means 'Enough!' as in 1 Samuel 15:16." That verse is part of the unhappy chapter where Saul has disobeyed the Lord and forfeited his right to the throne. In verse 16, Samuel interrupts Saul's justification for his actions by saying "Stop!" So when the psalmist uses the Hebrew phrase to tell us to "be still," he's in effect saying, "Stop! Concentrate! Shut everything else out of your mind and pay attention to Me!"

Another instance of God commanding His people to "be still" comes in Exodus, when Pharoah and his army are closing in on the escaping children of Israel, who apparently have no escape route. Moses tells the people, "The LORD will fight for you; you need only to be still." (Ex. 14:14) The idea of doing nothing when Pharoah and his military might are about to slaughter you doesn't easily comport with our desire for survival. Yet God's counter-intuitive command is the seemingly absurd instruction to do nothing, "be still." And why? As the psalmist records centuries later, the reason is "To *know* me." The experience of God parting the Red Sea to engineer their escape becomes the central memory in Israel's collective consciousness. This miracle shows the astonishing saving power of Yahweh, who obliterates the Egyptians. Also, by implication He shows the impotence of the Egyptians' pagan gods, who could do nothing to stop the Red Sea's waters from closing in on Pharoah and his troops.

In Nehemiah, when the Levites are about to instruct the people in the Word of God, we read, "The Levites calmed all the people, saying, 'Be still, for this is a holy day..."'" (Neh. 8:11) Here we have the sense of being quiet so that we can hear what's about to happen. Other translations have "be quiet," "be silent," or "hold your peace," the older equivalent found, not surprisingly, in the *King James Version*.

God desires that we don't only know *about* Him but know Him in the way we'd know our spouse or our child. ("Oh, I know him; he has such a sensitive nature that when his sister's upset he gets upset too.") We know our children's and our spouse's likes and dislikes, their character, what brings them joy. As we're invited in Psalm 46 to get to know God, we should draw on what we already know of God. J. B. Phillips says, "Let us remind ourselves then of the character of God, the methods of God, and the resources of God."[136] The more we get to know God, the deeper will be our understanding of *who* He is, *how* He works, and the *power* at His disposal.

But the word "know" in Hebrew has an additional dimension that's lacking in the English translation, that of sexual intimacy. We read in Genesis, for example, the *King James Version*, like many others, that "Adam knew Eve his wife; and she conceived, and bare Cain..."[137] The psalmist is therefore telling us here that God wants our relationship with Him to be as intimately loving as possible, commanding our fullest engagement.

To conclude, we are urged to "be still," to cease our movements and mobility. Doing so is not an end in itself but the necessary step for us to come closer to and expand our experience of God, that we may know Him even better on our journey today than we did yesterday.

---

[136] J. B. Phillips, *Making Men Whole*, 43.
[137] Gen. 4:1, *King James Version*. Other translations have "had relations with his wife," "made love to his wife," "was intimate with his wife," and so on.

Stumbling and Falling

Read Psalm 37:23-24

<u>*Key Verses:*</u> *"The LORD makes firm the steps of the one who delights in him; though he may stumble, he will not fall, for the LORD upholds him with his hand."* (Verses 23-24)

Eric Liddell was one of Scotland's greatest athletes, as we saw in **Running**.[138] (If you have not yet done so, please read that reflection now.) One additional moment early in the film is worth exploring here. Near the beginning of a 400-meter race, in an international meet, he is tripped and ends up sprawled on the ground. Seeing Liddell, played by Scottish actor Ian Charleson, lying there one can be excused for thinking, "Well, it's all over for him."

But that's not how Liddell sees it. He scrambles to his feet and resumes the race, making up a twenty-yard deficit to win the event. It's one of the film's most compelling scenes, showing the sheer grit and drive of the man—as well as his astonishing speed.

~~~~~

What are we to make of this episode of Liddell's stumble and subsequent recovery? An African proverb is helpful. It says, "Don't look where you fell, but where you slipped."[139] In other words, looking where you landed isn't helpful to prevent a fall next time. Instead, look at what made you fall. Was it an uneven sidewalk? A tree root? Or was it perhaps someone who either accidentally or deliberately tripped you?

Whatever the reason, you face two questions. First, how can I avoid this obstacle next time? Second, is there anything else I need to do as a result? Maybe you need to remove that problem root. Or if the school bully deliberately tripped you on the way to recess, some kind of further action is needed. For Liddell, the tripping and falling wasn't nearly as significant as his response: getting to his feet and resuming the race, pouring everything he could into it and emerging victorious despite his apparently race-ending tumble.

What about us? You know perfectly well what happened: On that

---

[138] This section on Eric Liddell is adapted from Gordon S. Jackson, *Ninety Days of Difference* and the analogy of the off-ramp is taken from Gordon S. Jackson, *Your Photo on God's Fridge Door*, 148-149.

[139] https://www.goodreads.com/quotes/1286445-do-not-look-where-you-fell-but-where-you-slipped. Accessed Oct. 6, 2024.

straight and narrow road that God has set before you, you let your attention wander and you drifted toward the road's shoulder, where the sound of tires on the rumble strip gave you a frightening warning that you were close to trouble. That time, you corrected the steering in a moment, averting the danger of a wreck. You recall how shaken you were, grateful for that safety measure, and all was well.

Or perhaps it was far worse. You weren't merely negligent; you suddenly yet willfully chose a tempting looking exit and left that straight and narrow road completely.[140] For whatever reason, you yielded impulsively to temptation on a biggy: you and a female colleague had too much to drink at a work conference and ended up in bed together; you hit a cyclist while driving home from work and, panic-stricken, drove off; you lost your temper and seriously hurt your four-year-old when he wouldn't stop whining. The point is, it's a big enough transgression against God, and those you've betrayed, to leave you drowning in guilt and convinced that God no longer wants anything to do with you. You hadn't planned this event but in that moment you succumbed to temptation. Now, you can't envision any way of getting back on that straight and narrow road. You tripped over temptation and fell as hard as you ever have.

It's precisely at that point, where you find yourself close to despair, that God miraculously provides out of nowhere an on-ramp back onto that highway you foolishly exited. God is the consummate road engineer. Regardless of the terrain, He is able instantly to pave the way for us to get back on track with Him.

We can picture Jesus scouring the landscape for any who've taken a wrong exit. "For the Son of Man came to seek and to save the lost." (Lk. 19:10) Whether we choose to use the new on-ramp created especially for us is another matter. Tragically, some who've strayed from God's highway opt never to return, even though like the father in the story of the Prodigal Son, God is always hoping, waiting for us to "come home."

There are probably others with whom we also need to reconcile, others who were hurt by our actions and possibly legal issues to face. But the emphasis here is on what we fear is a shattered relationship with God because of what we've done, something so egregious or life-changing that we fear we can never restore our relationship with Him. Philip Yancey offers a word of reassurance: "Grace means there is nothing we can do to make God love us more... and there is nothing we can do to make God love us less."[141]

As is so often the case, it is the psalmist who offers hope: both of a

---

[140] Compare this kind of impulsive temptation to the more deliberate steps taken toward sinning, as described in **Detours**.
[141] Philip Yancey, *What's So Amazing About Grace*, 70.

way out of your mess and of far better terrain in future: "He lifted me out of the slimy pit, out of the mud and mire; he set my feet on a rock and gave me a firm place to stand."[142]

Unlike a 100-meters or even a 400-meters event, the lifelong race set before us includes many more occasions when we're likely to stumble. We may fall through our own fault or perhaps because we were tripped. As we're lying there, perhaps after an especially painful fall, we may be tempted to say, "Enough! I quit." But then you hear Jesus beside you saying, "It's okay, I'm here. Let's get going again."

As you get to your grazed knees and Jesus helps you up, you tell Him you're no Eric Liddell; there's no way you're going to win this race after falling behind. Then he tells you you're defining "winning" the wrong way. "By the world's definition, I wasn't a winner. Yet in My Father's eyes I was, for finishing what I set out to do. Now, let's get to that finish line together."

~~~~~

"To him who is able to keep you from stumbling and to present you before his glorious presence without fault and with great joy – to the only God our Savior be glory, majesty, power and authority, through Jesus Christ our Lord, before all ages, now and forevermore! Amen." (Jude 24-25)

---

[142] Ps. 40:2.

Tents

Read Exodus 33:7-11

Key Verses: "Now Moses used to take a tent and pitch it outside the camp some distance away, calling it the 'tent of meeting.' Anyone inquiring of the LORD would go to the tent of meeting outside the camp. And whenever Moses went out to the tent, all the people rose and stood at the entrances to their tents, watching Moses until he entered the tent." (Verses 7-8)

When you see the word "tents," what comes to mind? Idyllic memories of family camping by the lake, with campfires, smores and perfectly still starlit nights? The circus? Or perhaps images of desperate refugees in Gaza in the thousands of tents supplied by the United Nations and other non-profit groups?

The Bible's interest in tents is extensive; they are mentioned more than 200 times. We can group the implications for our Christian journey into four categories. The first, and most obvious, is that tents refer to temporary accommodation. The second is that the tents represent a transient people. The third refers to the temporal bodies we inhabit. Finally, there's the tabernacle worship that sustained the children of Israel spiritually on their way to the Promised Land.

<u>Temporary Accommodation</u>: After leaving his ancestral home, Abraham and his family lived in tents. So did his descendants. This was at a time when other peoples had established towns and cities, with permanent homes. Abraham, by contrast, "... made his home in the Promised Land like a stranger in a foreign country; he lived in tents, as did Isaac and Jacob, who were heirs with him of the same promise." (Heb. 11:9) It's not as if Abraham couldn't afford to buy land or acquire settled accommodation; Genesis 13:2 describes him as a wealthy man, rich in livestock as well as silver and gold. Yet following God's leading, he fathered a nation of nomads — at least, until they had seized their freedom from the Egyptians and completed their wanderings through the desert. Until then, they had no settled habitation.

Even though a small number of societies are still nomadic and living out of tents, such as Bedouins, the vast majority of humankind live in settled accommodation. For most of us, tents represent either temporariness or the inability to afford permanent housing. We think of the homeless or refugees living in tents supplied by humanitarian organizations, living in desperate poverty and hoping for better and more permanent housing — *beyond-tent* housing. Those who go camping know that when their Memorial Day weekend or Fourth of July weekend is over, they'll pack their tents and head home to a dwelling that is as permanent as their tent was temporary.

Transient People: That "temporariness" applies both to tents themselves and to God's people. As far as our earthly existence is concerned, we are transient people. In the words of the song by Jim Reeves, "This world is not my home, I'm just a passing through..."[143] Christians who are not heavenly oriented in their life's journey risk undercutting their Christian commitment. "The only ultimate disaster that can befall us is to feel ourselves at home on this earth," says Malcolm Muggeridge.[144]

Spiritually speaking, we are "tent people." We need to think twice if we're considering settling down and packing the tent away in our newly acquired basement. As Barbara Moorman warns us, "It is curious to realize that people like you and me, who set such store by being settled and secure, should worship a God whose revelation was to nomads and wanderers. We try to domesticate God, try to get God to settle down with us — but never succeed."[145]

Temporal Bodies: Not only are we transient people, living in transient accommodation, we occupy our very bodies only on a temporary basis. Paul uses the image of our human bodies as tents, temporary dwelling places on this earthly journey. *The Message* says it well: "[W]e know that when these bodies of ours are taken down like tents and folded away, they will be replaced by resurrection bodies in heaven — God-made, not handmade — and we'll never have to relocate our 'tents' again." (2 Cor. 5:1-3) As the *NIV* study notes on these verses comment, "As a tent is a temporary and flimsy abode, so our bodies are frail, vulnerable and wasting away." Paul's focus was anticipating the new, spiritual body he would one day receive,[146] a resurrection body comparable to the one in which Jesus appeared to His followers from the Easter morning onwards. Peter echoes this theme of the body-as-tent, when he says, "I live in the tent of this body." (2 Pet. 1:13)

Not that Paul despised his current tent-like physical body. On the contrary, he spoke about our body as the temple of the Holy Spirit. (1 Cor. 6:19) This view was the polar opposite of the secular philosophers of his day, some of whom argued either for hedonism (eat, drink and be merry, indulging the pleasures of the body) or asceticism (strict self-discipline in

---

[143] Words and music by Albert E. Brumley (1905-1977), composed in 1919. In the public domain.
[144] Quotes in Gordon S. Jackson: *Quotes for the Journey, Wisdom for the Way*, 141.
[145] Ibid.
[146] See his comments in 1 Cor. 15:44.

one's eating and other practices affecting the body). The psalmist too views the body positively, noting the marvel of the human body: "I will praise thee; for I am fearfully and wonderfully made: marvelous are thy works..." (Ps. 139:14, *King James Version*) Yet even this marvelous body will be superseded one day by a resurrection body whose nature we cannot grasp. Our current "tent-like" body will fall away, to be replaced by something that theologians and philosophers struggle to explain.[147]

In short, we have a pilgrim body for the time being, a vehicle to travel our earthly journey. James Montgomery put it this way in his hymn, "At Home in Heaven":

Here in the body pent [confined, imprisoned]
Absent from Him I roam,
Yet nightly pitch my moving tent
A day's march nearer home.[148]

Tabernacle Worship: The assigned Bible reading for this reflection was chosen for a simple reason: whatever can be said about temporal accommodation, transient people, and temporal bodies, and their relationship to our faith journey, God is central to that journey. So is the significance of the tents He instructed Moses to erect as the children of Israel made their way through the wilderness. In fact, the first tent, known as "the tent of meeting," was placed outside the Israelite camp. It was followed later by the tabernacle, a more permanent but still portable structure placed at the heart of the camp. This elaborate structure accompanied the Israelites to the end of their journey.

The tent of meeting was the place where Moses interacted with God while the tabernacle was being built. That is where he received God's direction, including detailed instructions for the building of the tabernacle.[149] No sacrifices were offered at the tent of meeting; that role was reserved for the tabernacle, which was the venue for the various offerings and sacrifices that the Israelites brought to honor and worship God. In this way, the tabernacle foreshadowed the permanent temple that was built in Jerusalem. Both the tabernacle and the temple were seen as the venue where Yahweh resided; they were most holy places and were treated with utmost reverence.

What is the significance of the tent of meeting and the tabernacle for us today? Unlike the Israelites, we don't believe God dwells in one

---

[147] See for example Stephen T. Davis: *After We Die*, in which he describes some of the theories concerning the nature of our resurrection bodies.
[148] https://hymnary.org/text/forever_with_the_lord_amen_so_let_it_be. Accessed June 20, 2024.
[149] See Ex. 24-31.

particular place. We believe He is omnipresent and that as spirit He is present everywhere. More important, though, is the lesson the Israelites learned from the tabernacle. It was a physical reminder that God was not only present with them now but would also accompany them throughout their journey. They, in turn, needed to make a conscious commitment to carrying the tabernacle every time they relocated to the next step on their journey. They could have chosen to abandon the tabernacle, grumbling that it was too much of a hassle to keep moving it. We too may at times find our commitment to God too onerous and our relationship with God may be in jeopardy — or as in the parable of the sower and the seed, even wither and die. (Mt. 13)

Note too that the tabernacle was placed in the center of the Israelite camp (Nu. 2:17), signifying that Yahweh was at the heart of the Israelite community. Everything about their existence, their journeying forward, their identity as a nation: all this centered on this structure and Whose home it was. For us today, we too ought to have God at the center of all that we do, both now, and in our dependence on Him as we continue our journey, each day pitching our tents closer to home.

There Be Giants

Read Nu. 13:31-33

Key Verse: *"And there we saw the giants, the sons of Anak, which come of the giants: and we were in our own sight as grasshoppers, and so we were in their sight." (Verse 33,* King James Version)

So, what did you expect: that Christianity would be a problem-free ride? That it would all be plain sailing? Or to use yet another cliché, have no bumps in the road? Of course you should have expected problems along the way, perhaps as you tried to figure out your role on a secular college campus or in a secular office environment. Or maybe you've encountered surprising hostility or opposition from people you expected would be supportive, even family members. No matter the source, you're dealing with exactly the kinds of trials the apostle Peter discusses in his first epistle. As he puts it, "Dear friends, do not be surprised at the fiery ordeal that has come on you to test you, as though something strange were happening to you." (1 Pet. 4:12)

This is normal for the Christian life, as it was for the children of Israel en route to the Promised Land. Joshua and Caleb were among the twelve spies sent to check out the land and came back with a favorable report. But their recommendation to move ahead was overridden by the other ten, as we read in Numbers:

> *But the men that went up with him said, We be not able to go up against the people; for they are stronger than we. And they brought up an evil report of the land which they had searched unto the children of Israel, saying, The land, through which we have gone to search it, is a land that eateth up the inhabitants thereof; and all the people that we saw in it are men of a great stature. And there we saw the giants, the sons of Anak, which come of the giants: and we were in our own sight as grasshoppers, and so we were in their sight. (Nu. 13:31-33,* King James Version)

The sons of Anak, perceived to be the giants, were too much of a threat. So the Israelites were condemned to wandering the desert for decades more because of the reluctance of these ten men to trust in Yahweh, who had not only brought them to the brink of the Promised Land, but was ready to lead them to finish the journey.

As the devotional book, *Streams in the Desert*, puts it, "It is when we are in the way of duty that we find giants. It was when Israel was going

135

forward that the giants appeared. When they turned back into the wilderness they found none."[150]

So what giants are you facing today? Are you ready, with the help of the God Who has led you thus far, to move forward and face them head on? Or will you turn back, into a wilderness of your own, where you will find none?

---

[150] *Streams in the Desert*, 207.

Thin Places

Read Matthew 17:1-8

<u>Key Verses</u>: *"There he was transfigured before them. His face shone like the sun, and his clothes became as white as the light. Just then there appeared before them Moses and Elijah, talking with Jesus." (Verses 2-3)*

A "Thin Place" is an important concept in Celtic theology. It is understood as a place where the distance between heaven and earth is reduced to the point that you can clearly experience the divine. It's as if there's an especially thin veil between two worlds that, if not permitting actual movement between them, at least allows humans to more clearly sense a world beyond our own.

A recent discussion of this concept featured the Israeli town of Tzfat, high above the Sea of Galilee, by Eric Weiner, a travel journalist. Writing for the BBC, Weiner says that every time he visits Tzfat, "I feel an unexpected calm descend. It may not be heaven, not exactly, but the soft air and unhurried atmosphere lend a lightness to an otherwise heavy land."[151]

He describes how the town is steeped in the culture of Kabbalah, the mystical strain of Judaism, which in hard-to-explain ways instills in Tzfat "a vitality, a quirkiness." He continues, "Tzfat taught me how to sit still. Here, unlike so many other places, I never feel like I am missing something, that there is something 'better' out there. Tzfat made me realize that joy can be found in some unusual places."

Or even something other than joy. Think for example of Moses' encounter with God at the burning bush, or Joshua overlooking Jericho; in both instances they need to be reminded they are on holy ground. Or think of the disciples who were with Jesus at the transfiguration.

A thin place is by definition perceived by something other than our normal senses. Moreover, different people will perceive it differently, if at all. It may be that for you, a particular place provides a special, hard-to-define feeling every time you go there. It could be a place in the outdoors, especially somewhere isolated, or perhaps your church sanctuary or in a majestic cathedral. Weiner speaks of his experience when he notes that "… Thin Places are spiritual, but not conventionally so. A forest can be a thin place, and so can a library. Even bars or shopping malls can be Thin Places,

---

[151] https://www.bbc.com/travel/article/20151019-a-city-that-will-teach-you-to-be-at-peace. Accessed May 14, 2024.

though admittedly it's less likely. Similarly, not all 'spiritual' places are thin. Jerusalem, the 'city of peace,' fails to stir my soul."

A word of warning is in order, though. There's much about God and His dealings with us mortals of which we know little; the realm of mysticism is one such arena. Many of us have intensely personal spiritual experiences that we might regard as mystical, and which we would struggle to describe to anyone. But always it's important to keep ourselves grounded in good theology and biblical teaching or examples.

Two such examples come immediately to mind regarding Thin Places: Jesus' transfiguration and Moses' ineffable meetings with God. In Matthew's account of the transfiguration, Jesus' appearance is dramatically transformed; as we read, His "face shone like the sun, and his clothes became as white as the light." (Mt. 17:2) The three disciples who are with Jesus are completely overwhelmed by what they witness — a clearly supernatural, mysterious event that defied explanation, yet was clearly grounded in holiness.

A comparable holiness attended Moses, on numerous occasions. Exodus 3 tells of his first "Thin Place" meeting, on the occasion of his burning bush experience. As he encountered God, he was told he was standing on holy ground and must remove his sandals. Subsequently, we read in Exodus that "The LORD descended to the top of Mount Sinai and called Moses to the top of the mountain. So Moses went up…" (Ex. 19:20) Later still, we learn of his repeated meetings, presumably in the tabernacle, where he mysteriously met with Yahweh, and the effect it had on him: "[W]henever he entered the LORD's presence to speak with him, he removed the veil until he came out. When he came out and told the Israelites what he had been commanded, they saw that his face was radiant. Then Moses would put the veil back over his face until he went in to speak with the LORD." (Ex. 34:34-35)

In the reflection on **Limping** we read of Jacob's life-changing encounter with God, when he stays on one side of the Jabbok river after sending his entire party to the other side. He was alone and then wrestled with God the entire night.

Four observations are worth noting.

- First, God sometimes will appoint as a thin place a mountain top or some other remote area.
- Second, those who encounter God in such a place are typically alone, an exception being the transfiguration, where Jesus wanted Peter, James and John to witness the occasion.
- Third, God appears wherever He chooses. It could even be in the quiet of our living room as we're having a morning devotional.
- Fourth, these theophanies (God's appearances in some form to humans) are entirely at God's discretion. We don't get to order

up a theophany as if it were part of room service.

In other words, we shouldn't seek such moments. We should certainly not demand them or think if we spend time alone at our favorite place in the woods or sit quietly in a side chapel of a cathedral, that we can somehow entice God to appear to us in some form. These events, even in Scripture, are rare indeed. Instead, we should be careful to focus at all times on the person of Jesus Christ, the "author and finisher of our faith." (Heb. 12:2) If perhaps we have something like a theophany that enhances or enriches our relationship with Him, good and well. But anything that pulls us in another direction, however marvelous it may seem, should be shunned. As the Apostle John puts it, "Dear friends, do not believe every spirit, but test the spirits to see whether they are from God...." (1 Jn. 4:1)

Thin Places can be part of a legitimate Christian experience but one needs to ensure that experience is placed in a fuller context of one's faith.

The Celts would have agreed.

Traveling Companion

Read Exodus 33:14-15

<u>Key Verses</u>: *"Yahweh replied, 'I myself will go with you, and I will give you rest.' Moses said, 'If you are not going with us yourself, do not make us leave this place.'" (Verses 14-15,* Jerusalem Bible)

In this passage we have Moses telling God (1) that he has heard and understood the promise that God will accompany the Israelites until their journey's end, and (2) that there's no point going any further without God's divine presence. We know that Moses' motivation for saying what he does in Part 2 is not mere politeness, along the lines of, "Oh, come on, it won't be the same without you." No, at the very least Moses knows that without God's leadership and presence, the Israelites' journey is pointless. God alone, the One Who has called them out of Egypt and led them safely thus far, with one desert miracle after another beginning with the crossing of the Red Sea, can bring them safely to the Promised Land. Even if they were confident of making it past the hazards that undoubtedly lay ahead without God's help, Yahweh was their *God*; how could they possibly part ways and leave Him behind?

With us too, how can we even imagine continuing our life's journey by parting company with God? "Thanks, Lord, for everything so far. But I'm going to strike out on my own now." For anyone to think of turning one's back on God in that way is breathtaking. For those of us who, like the Israelites, have been rescued and redeemed from our equivalent of Egypt, to shrug off our God is beyond belief. How can we turn our back on the God of Whom hymn-writer Robert Grant says:

Your mercies, how tender, how firm to the end,
Our Maker, Defender, Redeemer, and Friend![152]

Moses affirms that there's no point going forward without the presence of Yahweh, knowing that God's mercies will be with them until the end of their journey. Nor will those mercies cease when the Israelites reach Canaan. It's the same for you. Whatever your journey holds for today, tomorrow or next year, you have the assurance that God will lead and accompany you. Moreover, you've walked with God long enough to know there'd be no point continuing your faith journey on your own and leaving behind your maker, defender, redeemer and friend.

---

[152] "O Worship the King," Robert Grant, 1833. In the public domain.

Waiting

Read Psalm 27:14

Key Verse: "Wait for the LORD; be strong and take heart and wait for the LORD." (Verse 14)

We've heard the expression, "Watching paint dry." The account in 2 Samuel 10 points us to a real life incident that led to a comparable kind of waiting: watching beards grow. The story involves David's emissaries who were sent to the new (and young and foolish) king of the Ammonites, to convey David's condolences on the death of his father. Instead of receiving them with the dignity befitting a diplomatic entourage, he was easily persuaded that the envoys were on a spy mission. So he shaved half their beards and cut off their clothes so their buttocks were exposed. Both of these actions were grave insults, which led to a war with the Ammonites.

When David learned what happened, he sent a message to the men. Sensitive to their deep humiliation, he said: "Stay at Jericho till your beards have grown, and then come back." (2 Sam.10:5) The men had to spend their days, in quasi-exile, waiting for their beards to grow to their previous length. Theirs was an unexpected time of waiting. It was also unproductive; when they could have been actively engaged in David's service, these men were sidelined.

Others wait for God's direction, also seemingly sidelined because God seems silent. E. M. Blaiklock wrote, "Time-bound man chafes at God's long delays. 'O Lord, make haste to help us,' is the most human of man's prayers."[153] Many Christians would agree. Waiting for God's leading is extraordinarily difficult, unnatural, and yet always worthwhile. Admittedly, waiting for God's leading is one of the most difficult aspects of our Christian walk. But wait we must. Christians throughout the ages have learned that we dare not rush God. He works according to His timetable and if we are serious about seeking His purposes in our lives, we need to fit in with His way of doing things.

Sometimes we face a tight deadline when we must decide something in a hurry. Most often, though, the problem is merely our impatience. We *want* to decide soon, largely because we want to *know* our next step. Like children on a long car trip, we keep asking Mom or Dad, "When will we be there? How much longer?" It seems Moms and Dads always give the

[153] E. M. Blaiklock, *Bible People*, 26.

same kind of vague answers that we get from God: "Soon" or "A little while yet." Yet, as we know from the car rides of our childhood, we do eventually reach our destinations. The problem was never whether we'd arrive where we were going, as much as it was our impatience on the journey.

Waiting is similar to the **Doldrums**, in that nothing seems to be happening. But waiting is a more specific condition rather than the general malaise that characterizes the Doldrums. We normally are waiting for concrete things like answers to specific prayers (slow, slow healing as you try to recover from long Covid or a protracted season of unemployment, for example, or perhaps an aching to find your life partner). Other aspects of your faith journey may be in good shape. You don't have a case of what we could call the "systemic spiritual blahs," it's only in this one area where God seems inactive.

We may be in waiting mode for several reasons. One is that God isn't ready to act in our situation or respond to our prayers. Maybe He's putting various things in place before He can show us what the next steps are. A second reason is that *we* are not ready for the next step and God is wisely holding us back until the moment is ripe. Sometimes our situation may be so complex that it needs time to percolate or mature, and we'd be foolish to move to a premature next step. Other times the reason for waiting may be a mystery. We cannot see why God seems to have put our petitions in a "call waiting" queue. It seems our faith journey is on hold, for no apparent reason.

Of course, we aren't the first to notice that God seems to delay, without apparent reason. The various authors of the psalms touched on this issue time and again, with a mix of lament at how long it was taking God to act, as well as unstinting confidence and trust in God. Here are ten examples in which the psalmist pours out his soul to God:

- My soul is in deep anguish. How long, LORD, how long? Turn, LORD, and deliver me... (Ps. 3:4-5)
- In the morning, LORD, you hear my voice; in the morning I lay my requests before you and wait expectantly. (Ps. 5:3)
- How long, LORD? Will you forget me forever? How long will you hide your face from me? (Ps. 13:1)
- Wait for the LORD; be strong and take heart and wait for the LORD. (Ps. 27:14)
- We wait in hope for the LORD; he is our help and our shield. (Ps. 33:20)
- How long, Lord, will you look on? (Ps. 35:17)
- I waited patiently for the LORD; he turned to me and heard my cry. (Ps. 40:1)
- For God alone I wait silently; my deliverance comes from him.

(Ps. 62:1, *Revised English Bible*)

- How long must your servant wait? (Ps. 119:84)
- I wait for the LORD, my whole being waits, and in his word I put my hope. (Ps. 130:5)

~~~~~

How will God evaluate the way we handled our waiting time? Will we come through this time with patience and a quiet reliance on Him? Or will it be with an attitude of checking our watches every few minutes and an irritation that signals our displeasure with how God is going about His business?

PART 3: Wrapping Up

Conclusion

Read Psalm 32:8

<u>Key Verse</u>: *"I shall teach you and guide you in the way you should go. I shall keep you under my eye..." (Verse 8,* Revised English Bible)

~~~~~

"O God, who brought Abraham your son out of the land of the Chaldees, and preserved him unhurt through all his journeying, we beseech you to keep us your servants safe; be to us our support in setting out, our solace on the way, our shade in the heat, our shelter in the rain and cold, our transport in our weariness, our fortress in trouble, our staff in slippery paths, our harbor on stormy seas, that under your guidance we may safely reach our destination, and at length return home in safety."

-- *The Book of Catholic Prayer*[154]

~~~~~

It is difficult to imagine a more comprehensive prayer to equip and sustain us on our Christian journey. Everything is there, from seeking guidance as we set out, to the needs for solace and safety, and an ability to cope with slippery paths and stormy seas. In one way or another, the prayer touches on every topic we've looked at in this book.

We have considered the nature of biblical journeys and looked at how diverse they are. Some journeys end with people reaching their destinations, sometimes not. Similarly, we notice various interruptions of the postures represented in Scripture. What should be our posture at any given moment? It all depends, as E. M. Blaiklock says, citing Moses' example: "There are times, as Moses knew, to 'be still and know that I am God.' There are also times to be up and doing."[155]

So, sometimes we are to sit and wait, other times we are to be running, even soaring, as we move toward the destination God has in mind for us. He prepares our way and anticipates our commitment to sticking with the journey, in fair weather and foul, whether we are soaring or stumbling. Christians should embrace the wisdom of a Nigerian proverb that says, "Keep your eyes on your destination and not on where you stumbled."[156]

---

[154] Quoted in Gordon S. Jackson: *The Weather is Here, Wish You Were Beautiful: Quotations for the Thoughtful Traveler,* 137.

[155] E. M. Blaiklock: *Commentary on the Psalms,* 91.

[156] Annetta Miller: *African Wisdom for Life,* May 3.

~~~~

We began this section with words from one prayerbook. Let us end with words from another: "May Christ's holy, healing, enabling Spirit be with you every step of the way, and be your guide as your road changes and turns."[157]

---

[157] *New Zealand Prayer Book*, 542.

Acknowledgements

The English poet John Donne famously wrote that "No man is an island..." We don't exist or live our lives independent of others. We all need each other. And while writing is initially a solo endeavor, the polishing and editing benefits greatly from the input of others. This book has been shaped by these loyal and helpful friends, who have contributed significantly to polishing and refining *Sit, Stand, Walk, Run*: Dennis Butler, Malcolm De Kock, Jeff Haschick, Dia Maurer, and Gregg Sealey. I am most grateful to them, as well as to Michelle Levigne, Mount Zion Ridge Press's copy editor, for catching those recalcitrant errors that the rest of us missed.

About the Author

Gordon S. Jackson is a South African-born educator and author. He grew up in Cape Town, where he received his undergraduate education. He then completed an MA at Wheaton College in Illinois and worked as a reporter and editor for a newsmagazine in Johannesburg.

Returning to the United States, he then completed his doctorate in mass communication at Indiana University in 1983. He then began his teaching career at Whitworth University, a liberal arts institution in Spokane, WA. He retired in 2015 but has remained active as an author.

Sit, Stand, Walk, Run is his twenty-first book. In addition to two scholarly books, he has written three satirical novels, an anthology of satirical pieces about the church, and several other faith-related books.

He is married to another South African, who helps to keep his accent honest. He and his wife have two adult children and identical twin granddaughters.

THANK YOU!

Thank you for reading this book from Mt. Zion Ridge Press.

If you enjoyed the experience, learned something, gained a new perspective, or made new friends through story, could you do us a favor and write a review on Goodreads or wherever you bought the book?

Thanks! We and our authors appreciate it.

We invite you to visit our website, MtZionRidgePress.com, and explore other titles in fiction and non-fiction. We always have something coming up that's new and off the beaten path.

And please check out our podcast, **Books on the Ridge,** where we chat with our authors and give them a chance to share what was in their hearts while they wrote their book, as well as fun anecdotes and glimpses into their lives and experiences and the writing process. And we always discuss a very important topic: *Tea!*

You can listen to the podcast on our website or find it at most of the usual places where podcasts are available online. Please subscribe so you don't miss a single episode!

Thanks for reading. We hope you come back soon!

www.ingramcontent.com/pod-product-compliance
Lightning Source LLC
Chambersburg PA
CBHW011238120626
46549CB00009B/3323